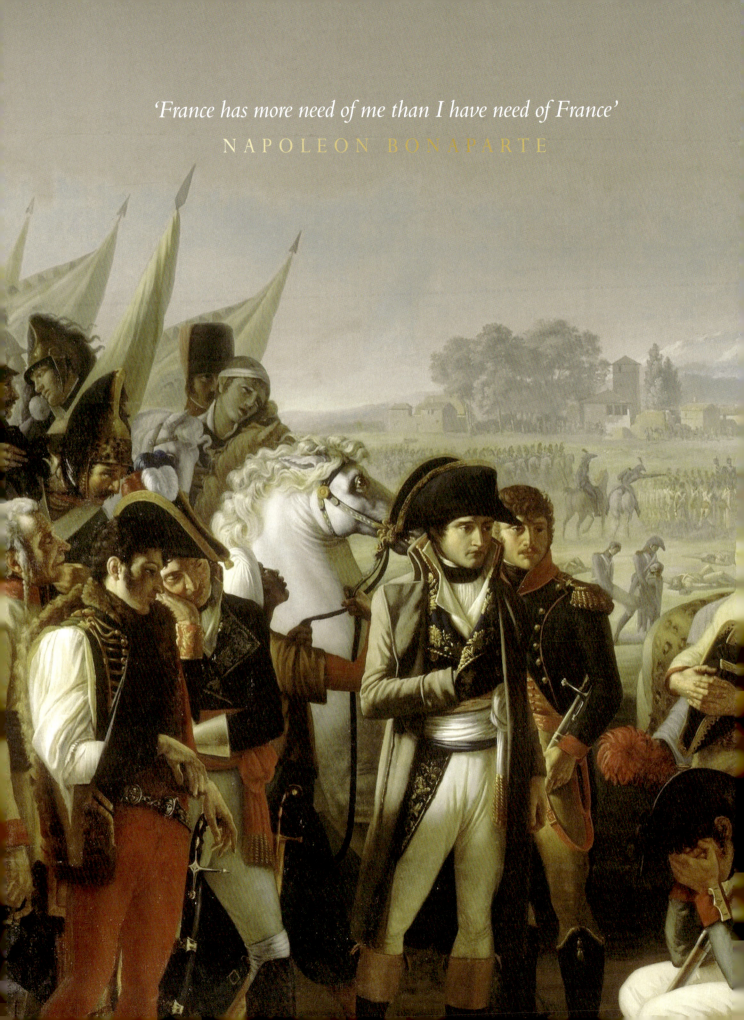

'France has more need of me than I have need of France'
NAPOLEON BONAPARTE

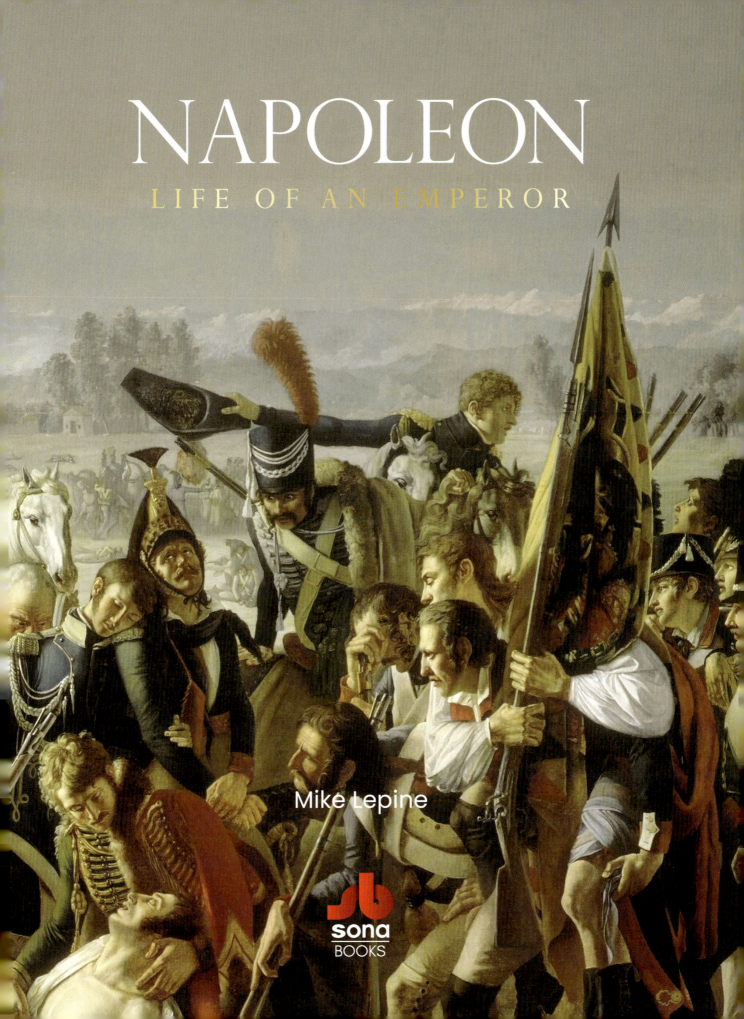

NAPOLEON
LIFE OF AN EMPEROR

Mike Lepine

sb sona BOOKS

sona BOOKS

© Danann Media Publishing Limited 2023

First Published Danann Media Publishing Limited 2023
WARNING: For private domestic use only, any unauthorised Copying, hiring, lending or public performance of this book is illegal.

CAT NO: SON0580

Images as credited

Book design Darren Grice at Ctrl-d

Copy editors & Proof readers Tom O'Neill and Juliette O'Neill

All rights reserved. No Part of this title may be reproduced or transmitted in any material form (including photocopying or storing it in any medium by electronic means and whether or not transiently or incidentally to some other use of this publication) without the written permission of the copyright owner, except in accordance with the provisions of the Copyright, Designs and Patents Act 1988. Applications for the copyright owner's written permission should be addressed to the publisher.

Made in EU.
ISBN: 978-1-915343-42-0

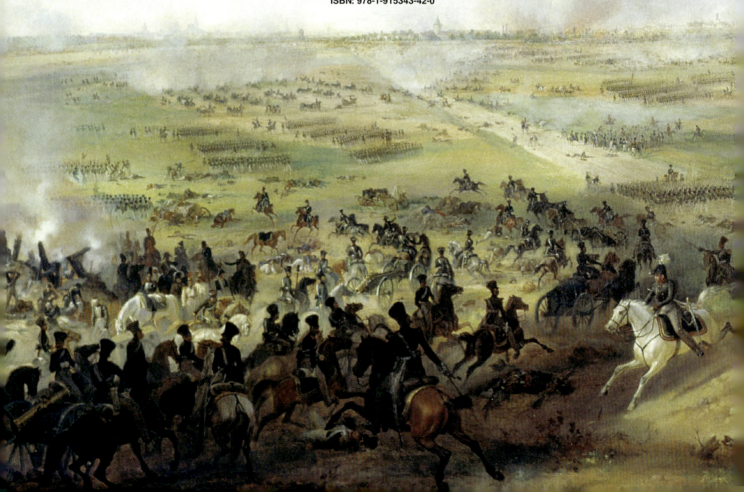

CONTENTS

THE LITTLE CORPORAL	8
TERROR & OPPORTUNITY	16
SEIZING POWER	44
THE NAPOLEONIC WARS	60
DECLINE & FALL	96
THE ONE HUNDRED DAYS	108

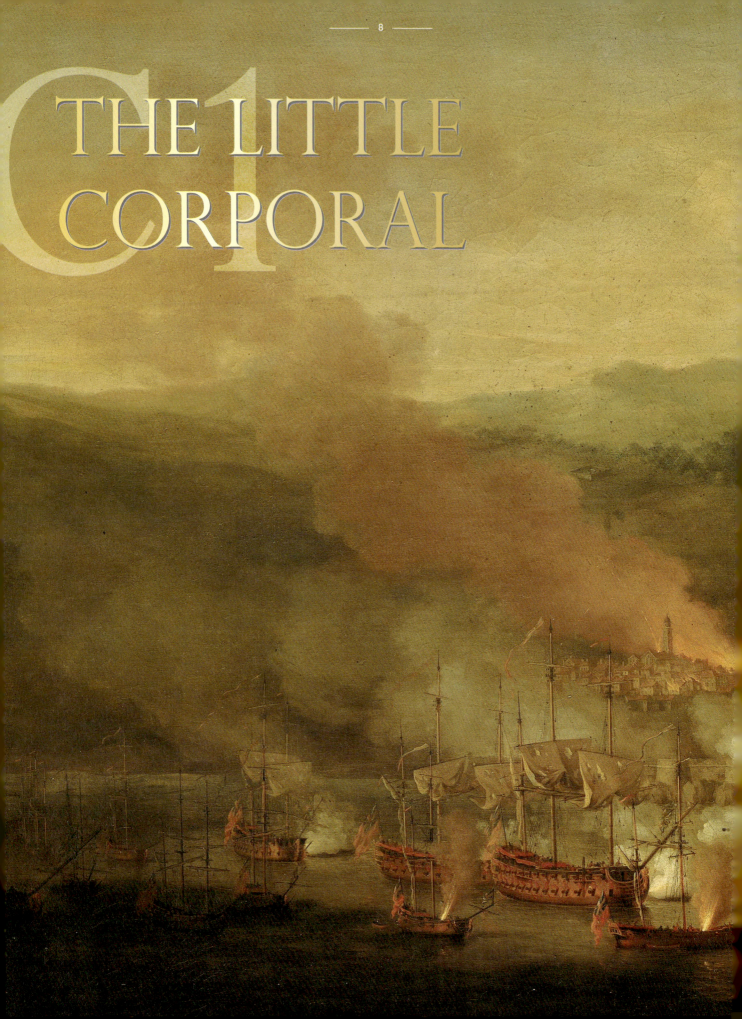

CHAPTER 1
THE LITTLE CORPORAL

THE (VERY) LITTLE CORPORAL

'(The young Napoleon) was the perfect little savage'
Carl Jung

In 1769, the Mediterranean island of Corsica was little more than a waste of dry land an inconvenient distance off the west coast of Italy. Much of it was dauntingly mountainous, and that which wasn't comprised some of Europe's most outstanding scrubland. What civilisation there was could be found huddled in the towns along the coast. The interior belonged exclusively to deeply superstitious and vendetta-driven bandit clans and violent radical nationalist groups. Periodically, one or the other would swoop down on one of the coastal towns, raid it for booty and then disappear back into the mountains.

Even in a time of frantic empire building, no-one really wanted to rule the island. Nominally, it had been controlled by the Italian city state of Genoa since 1284, but in reality that control only extended to the coast. Inland, the wild towns and villages proved impossible to police. The British seized Corsica twice in the 18th century only to somewhat sheepishly give it back on both occasions. Corsica could not be exploited because it had nothing to exploit. In 1755, the island declared independence from Genoa. It didn't last. After getting France to help them crush the rebellion, Genoa practically begged the French to take the island off their hands for good and France finally annexed Corsica in 1769.

Thus it was that, when baby Napoleone Buonaparte was born in Ajaccio, one of the largest coastal towns on Corsica, on 15 August 1769, he automatically qualified as French, despite his name being Italian.

Napoleon was born the fourth child of twelve to Carlo Mario Buonaparte and his wife Maria Letizia. The family were minor old Tuscan nobility, wealthy enough to have a four storey home and servants but not wealthy enough to be consistently comfortable and idle. At home, the Bonapartes spoke a mixture of Corsican and Italian. Napoleon's father worked as a lawyer. He was quiet and vague, a hopeless gambler

and forever dreaming up get-rich-quick schemes (He was intending to branch out into breeding Silkworms when he died). Letizia, however, was an entirely different character. She was fierce, passionate, devoutly religious and quite sarcastic and cynical. It was widely believed that Letizia's family had, over the centuries, interbred with the wild bandits of the interior and that was from where she had inherited her fiery personality. One contemporary described her as *'easily the most striking woman in Ajaccio.'* Throughout her life, she never took her son Napoleon's ambitions or achievements seriously and was forever warning him that it could all collapse tomorrow. As a child, his parents nicknamed him *Rabulione*, which means *'he who meddles in everything.'*

The infant Napoleon was short, sullen and solitary, bothering with the children around him only when he had commands to bark at them. He also bit other children. He disliked hanging around the house and ventured outdoors whenever he could. In Ajaccio Harbour, he stood for hours watching British warships as they came visiting and even dreamed of one day being in service to the Royal Navy. Only his mother could hope to control him.

'Nothing pleased me. I feared no one. I fought with one, kicked another, scratched a third, and made myself feared by all. My brother Joseph was my slave. My mother had to restrain my bellicose temper. Her tenderness was severe. She punished and rewarded indiscriminately.'

Napoleon

The young Napoleon Bonaparte studying at the military academy at Brienne-le-Chateau, France, circa 1780

SCHOOLDAYS

'With my sword by my side and Homer in my pocket, I hope to carve my way through the world.'
Napoleon in a letter home from school

At the age of five, Napoleon was sent to a Catholic boarding school in Ajaccio, where he proved particularly gifted at mathematics. Eager for their son to advance, the Bonaparte's saw to it that he started learning French at the age of seven. That, they decided - despite both being Francophobes and Corsican nationalists - was the future. Unfortunately, the little Corsican found the French language very difficult to get to grips with.

For a family with more ambition than money, it must have seemed like a miracle when both Napoleon and his brother Joseph suddenly became the recipients of a fund which granted scholarships to the children of hard-up nobility, which were intended to set them on a path to be either soldiers or clerics. Napoleon's parents had always intended for him to be a lawyer, but this was too good an opportunity to miss and they accepted his future would be that of a soldier. The scholarships were sorted out by the island's effective ruler, the Comte de Marbeuf. It is believed in some quarters that he did this because he fancied Napoleon's mother and hoped that his largesse would get her into bed. Opinion is still divided about whether his 'sex for scholarships' scheme ever bore wicked fruit.

In January 1779, at the age of nine, Napoleon and his brother Joseph were both despatched to the French mainland. Napoleon first found himself sent to a religious prep school at Autun where the head of primary education, Abbé Chardon, recalled him thus:

' (He was a) thoughtful character. He was interested in no one, and found his amusements by himself. He rarely had a companion in his walks. He was quick to learn, and quick of apprehension in all ways. When I gave him a lesson, he fixed his eyes upon me with parted lips; but if I recapitulated anything I had said, his interest was gone, as he plainly showed by his manner. When reproved for this, he would answer coldly, I might almost say with an imperious air, 'I know it already, sir.'

A few months later, Napoleon won a scholarship to the military academy at Brienne-le-Chateau near Troyes. Despite being a military school, the academy was run by monks. Napoleon was not happy. He still hated the French for their brutal treatment of the Corsican people when they crushed the island's independence. Worse, his French classmates saw him as a yokel, an idiot peasant from the provinces and teased him mercilessly. It didn't help that Napoleon still had great difficulty in reading or writing in French, and spoke with a thick Corsican accent that was to stay with him all his life. He was mocked as a *'scholarship boy'* and his tormentors also thought that he looked funny and unusually dark skinned. On admission he was just four feet ten inches tall. Children of the French aristocracy grew a lot taller. Napoleon responded by hurling back insults, and confrontations often descended into fist fights.

Given the teasing and taunting, it was hardly surprising that Napoleon made no good friends at the academy and retreated into solitude once more. While his fellow students revelled and drank, Napoleon shut himself away and studied hard. He could be a good scholar when he tried, but he would only apply himself to the subjects he liked such as maths, geography and history. When outside, he devoted himself to his allotment, skilfully transforming it into a pleasant garden where he might read under the bowers. His early love of gardening was to remain with him for life.

His school report from 1783 described him as:

'…very regular in his conduct, has always distinguished himself by his interest in mathematics. He has a sound knowledge of history and geography. He is very poor at dancing and drawing. He will make an excellent sailor.'

After five long years, Napoleon finally graduated from the academy and progressed to the École Militaire in Paris along with a reference describing him thus: *'Character masterful, impetuous and headstrong.'*, The École Militaire was a shock to Napoleon. His old academy had been Spartan, but at his new college the facilities were luxurious and the young men enjoyed five course meals. Never particularly enamoured of food, Napoleon disapproved of such self-indulgence. If the college disconcerted him, the grand city of Paris absolutely overawed him and he was reported to be seen wandering the streets, gawping at all the opulent sights. He graduated in 1785, having specialised in the artillery, and ranked a dismal 42nd out of 58 in his year. He was still just 16-years old.

Napoleon's father had died from stomach cancer in 1785, leaving virtually nothing in his will, and his son was consequently forced by lack of funds to complete the two year course at the École Militaire in just one year. In addition all the extra study, Napoleon now found himself at the head of the large Bonaparte family at the tender age of fifteen. Generous by nature, he used up much of his pay of 93 livres a month to keep his mother and siblings from going hungry. The responsibility plunged him into near poverty.

École Militaire, Paris

'Do you know how I managed ? By never entering a cafe or going into society; by eating dry bread and brushing my own clothes so they might last the longer. I lived like a bear, in a little room, with books for my only friends and when, thanks to abstinence, I had saved up a few crowns, I rushed off to the bookseller's shop and visited his coveted shelves ... These were the joys and debaucheries of my youth.' – Napoleon

INTO THE MILITARY

After Napoleon graduated he wanted to use his specialism in artillery to become a naval gunnery officer, but was too young to get a post. Instead he was commissioned into the La Fère artillery regiment as a second lieutenant. Despite having a good reputation, the regiment suffered from the increasing shortage of money afflicting France. Soldiers were obliged to sleep two to a small bed and they counted themselves lucky, as until quite recently it had been three to a bed. Pay was low. One of Napoleon's first tasks as a gunner was to help quell desperate food riots in Lyon. For pleasure, he read voraciously, preferring politics and philosophy over matters military. His reading reinforced his disenchantment with kings and priests.

'A STRONG JUST MAN'

In 1791, he requested extended leave and returned to Corsica to become involved in its struggle for liberation, convinced that liberation could only be achieved by a *'strong just man.'* His lofty ambition was to be that man, although he wrote at the time how much he hated ambition, describing it *'with its pale complexion, wild eyes, hurried footsteps, jerky gestures and sardonic laugh.'* And this from the most ambitious man in Europe. He spent several years getting caught up in messy politics, finding himself almost court-marshalled for anti-French activities and only succeeded in making a sworn enemy of the leader of the independence movement he had joined, Pasquale Paoli. Paoli had hated Napoleon's father for being too soft on the French and now he hated the son. An order was given to take Napoleon, dead or alive. In June 1793, Napoleon's mother and his brothers and sisters were forced to flee the island and settle in France where they hoped they were safe, while Napoleon turned French guns on the capital of Corsica before fleeing too for France, having been condemned to *'perpetual execration and infamy'*. His family's properties were destroyed, their lands and good seized. Napoleon became somewhat disenchanted with Corsica…

Napoleon in the Garrison at Auxonne with his Brother Louis

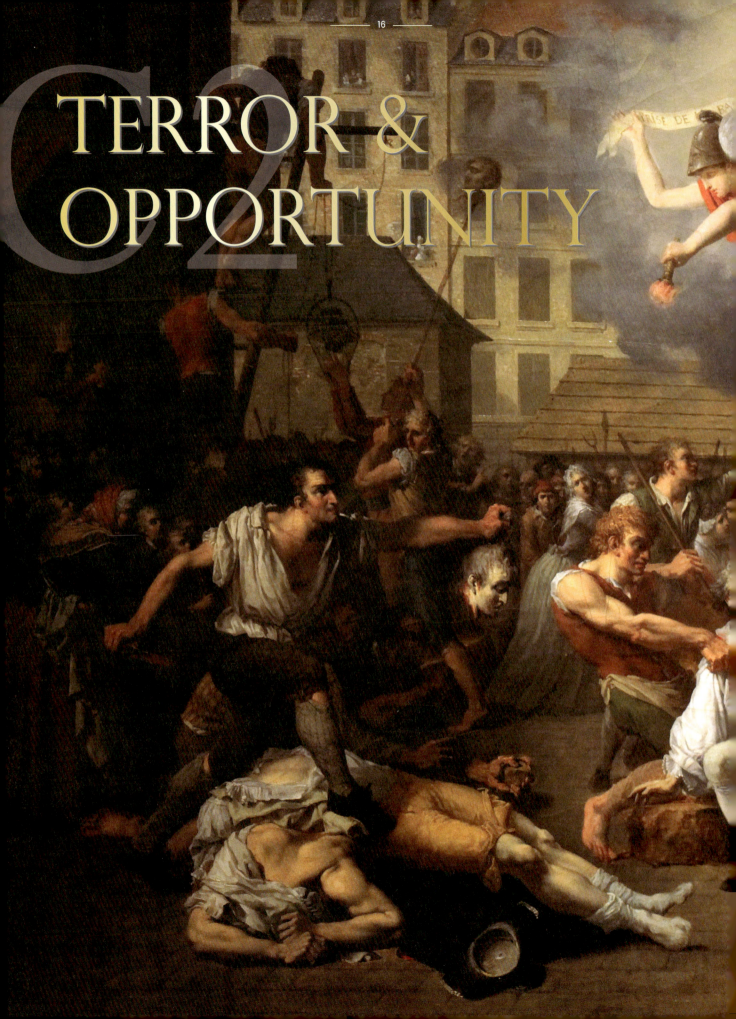

C2 TERROR & OPPORTUNITY

THINGS FALL APART

Things were changing in France. The nation was coming apart. The old Bourbon monarchy was slowly but surely losing its grip on power and the existing social order was under increasing pressure. There were serious financial problems too at almost all levels of the nation. Too much had been spent on keeping France grand and martial, and consequently state debt was swelling to unmanageable levels. Inflation hit food particularly hard, and a succession of poor harvests just made things worse. Now hunger was turning to starvation amongst the poor. The first food riots began. The very state teetered. The monarchy tried to impose more taxes to stabilise the economy, but these proved hugely unpopular with the French elite. King Louis XVI was not indifferent to reform, but was too weak to withstand the more conservative elements in his court. The aristocracy found themselves with diminishing power and influence – and with that, Napoleon understood, could come hitherto impossible opportunities for an ambitious young not-really-French, not-really-nobility soldier with a very keen eye for an opportunity and just a soupcon of patience...

King Louis XVI of France

A contemporary illustration of the Women's March on Versailles

The last hours of the French royal family (Louis XVI and Marie Antoinette) in the Louvre before the onset of the revolutionaries

TERROR & OPPORTUNITY

Inauguration of the States General, May 5, 1789

Order of the Lieutenant General in the Sénéchaussée and presidential headquarters of Lyon concerning the convocation of the Estates General of February 17, 1789

REVOLUTION AND TERROR

'Ability is nothing without opportunity'
Napoleon

As it became obvious that the monarchy could no longer run the nation, the Estates General was established for the first time in nearly two hundred years. This was a form of parliament representing the interests of the clergy, the aristocracy and the peasantry. It had been summoned by Louis XVI himself, but he soon came to regret his decision.

He wanted to talk taxes and new ways of raising revenue, but his assembly had far broader social reforms in mind. Consequently he banned them from the building they were meant to occupy. Undaunted the assembly held its first meeting on a tennis court in Versailles and committed themselves to forging a new constitution. In time, they became the Constituent Assembly.

The revolution proper began on 14 July 1789. Worried by rumours that the king would set his Swiss Guard on assembly members, the mob surged out into the streets of Paris to support them. French troops sent to stop the mob instead joined them. Together they stormed and seized the Bastille – an old prison and a symbol of royal tyranny (and most important of all a very well stocked armoury.) The prison governor's head ended up on a pole. Things rapidly started spiralling out of control. A former French finance minister was strung up along with his son. In the countryside, peasants started forming their own militias. The assembly was almost as alarmed as the monarchy at the burgeoning violence and tried to enact drastic social reforms, but it was far too late now. There were food riots in Paris itself and the king was forced to flee Versailles as a mob ransacked his palace. The following year, troops mutinied in Nancy. Louis XVI tried to escape to Austria in disguise, but was recognised and held against his will in Paris. Now there was a serious clamour to declare France a republic and to end the monarchy. Pro-Republican mobs met loyal troops and massacre was inevitable. More and more of the soldiery mutinied, leading to skirmishes between rogue French forces and the still-loyal Swiss Guard. In September 1791, as many as 1600 prisoners in French jails were murdered in case they harboured revolutionary sympathies. Most were just common criminals. On 10 August 1792, it was decided to 'temporarily suspend' the monarchy but in reality it was the beginning of the end for Louis XVI and his supporters.

A 1789 French hand tinted etching that depicts the storming of the Bastille during the French Revolution

TERROR & OPPORTUNITY

Storming of the Bastille and arrest of the Governor de Launay, July 14, 1789

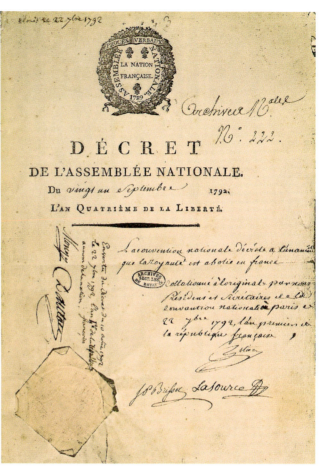

Dispatch of the decree taken by the Convention during its first session and abolishing royalty, signed by Pétion, president, Brissot and Lasource, session secretaries

Meanwhile, a National Convention was set up to run the country, but it was heavily divided between moderate and more radical elements. The Convention swiftly decided that 1792 should be renamed the glorious 'Year One' to deliberately affront Christianity and set about putting the king on trial. By January 1793, it had decided that Louis was guilty of *'conspiracy against public liberty and general safety'*; He was executed by guillotine before a vast crowd in the Place de la Concorde just a few days later. Less than a month after the execution, France declared war on Britain and the Netherlands in response to their criticism of the direction France was taking. It was already at war with Prussia, Sardinia and Austria. Conscription measures led to mass rioting and parts of the country rose up in open revolt. Some wanted the restoration of the monarchy. Others supported the broad idea of Republicanism but hated the Convention, which had started coming apart with the extremists gaining the ascendency.

Louis XVI with his confessor Edgeworth, a moment before his death on January 21, 1793

Etching, execution of Louis XVI

THE TERROR

'What constitutes the Republic is the complete destruction of everything that is opposed to it'
Louis Antoine de Saint-Just

'Clemency is barbarous'
Maximilien Robespierre

'We have already discovered four gaming-houses where people address each other as Monsieur and Madame'
Stanislas Freron, the 'Butcher of Toulon', describing the vile corruption in Marseilles

Louis Antoine de Saint-Just

In mid-1793, the National Convention established the Committee for Public Safety, which unwittingly gave the more lunatic and murderous elements in French politics a new power base. Thus began what became known as *'The Terror'*. The extremist elements of the Jacobite left cracked down on all opposition with a fervour and savagery that the monarchy could never have envisaged. Vigilante revolutionary gangs stalked the streets looking for anyone who looked like they might be an enemy of the revolution. In just nine months, a total of 16,600 *'enemies of freedom'* were imprisoned and then summarily executed. It's believed that up to another 40,000 never made it as far as gaol.. Between November 1793 and February 1794, over 4,000 prisoners were drowned in the Seine to save the cost of shooting them. It's said that, between 1793 and 1796, as many as 117,000 French men and women might have died in the Terror.

Much of early 1794 was devoted to the arrest and killing of prominent political dissidents. Then the Committee started spreading its net wider. In June 1794, those charged with counter revolutionary activities were denied all right to a defence. They were simply gathered up, taken to Paris and executed. Head of the Terror in the role of 'Public Accuser', Maximilien Robespierre, an ex-lawyer, included amongst his closest associates (whom were called the 'Twelve Just Men') a psychopath, a pornographer who had run off with his mother's silver, and a self-obsessed rake. It was also rumoured that Robespierre claimed that he was 'the second messiah.' While very probably somewhat lacking in divinity, he was certainly very short (he had to wear platform shoes), murderous, loved to hear himself talk (he made over 900 speeches) and determined to start his own religion, which he called *'The Cult of the Supreme Being'*. Pregnant and breastfeeding

TERROR & OPPORTUNITY

Engraving entitled The Arrest of Robespierre, 'The Night of the 9th to 10th Thermidor, Year II, 27th July 1794'

women were marched through the streets in celebration of this new Supreme One. Meanwhile, the clergy were thrown out of Notre Dame and replaced by prostitutes. Now, Robespierre himself came under increasing criticism and more moderate politicians realised, if they did not strike against him soon, he was liable to have them all executed…

Maximilien Robespierre

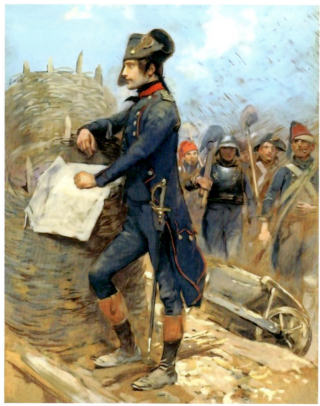

Bonaparte at the siege of Toulon, canvas by Édouard Detaille, 1793

BONAPARTE SHRUGGED

All this Napoleon lived through from a distance. He had no real interest in revolution or counter revolution. He cared not for the poor and, although he thought it was wrong to execute the king, he had no affection for the monarchy either. Napoleon was not a political beast. All that Napoleon cared about was Napoleon.

He had seen action, first as a loyal French officer at Auxonne in April 1789, when he led troops with bayonets fixed against a revolutionary mob. In July 1789, French officers became obliged to take an oath of allegiance to the National Assembly instead of the monarch. Many refused, considering it the act of traitor. Napoleon wasn't much bothered and took the oath readily on 4 July.

When Royalist forces aided by British troops seized the port of Toulon in the early autumn of 1793, it was Napoleon who was given the job of its recapture, even though there were far more high ranking officers present. Perhaps they secretly harboured divided

General du Teil

loyalties. In any event, Napoleon and his forces took Toulon back on 16 December. Not only did he command the artillery but also led the charge against the earthwork defences. He received a pike wound in the action and almost lost a leg. As he recuperated, the reprisals began. Robespierre's cronies hunted down 'traitors' with a passion . They had 200 officers and men from the French artillery shot merely on suspicion. Two days later another 200 civilians – men and women – were also shot. One government official announced ecstatically, *'We are shedding much impure blood, but for humanity…'*

Fulsome praise was heaped upon Napoleon for his action. General du Teil told Paris, *I lack words to list Bonaparte's merits'*. His only fault, he said was that he had *'too much courage.'* Napoleon was rewarded with promotion to the rank of Brigadier General. He was still only 24 years old.

DANGEROUS FRIENDS

Napoleon moved on to reorganise French artillery in preparation for a forthcoming invasion of Italy. It just so happened that his most ardent sponsor (and army commissioner) happened to be Augustin de Robespierre, the younger brother of the leader of the Terror. Dazzled by Napoleon's *'transcendent merit'*, Augustin Robespierre (nicknamed Bonbon') intended his protégé for ever greater things – until history intervened.

On July 1794, Maximilien Robespierre got his long overdue comeuppance and was guillotined. He had become crazier and crazier, and more and more murderous. An old lady was arrested, having been found with two penknives in her possession close to Robespierre's home. She, her parents and fifty-two others were executed for being part of what Robespierre had decided was an assassination attempt by the British. He talked of being the *'slave of liberty'* and threatened to poison himself. He started having frantic screaming fits against his fellow politicians and – their lives now in peril – they finally decided to act. He and four of his cronies were threatened with arrest. The revolutionary zealots Robespierre was banking on to rescue him failed to materialise, possibly because it was raining. Deciding to take his liberty (to which he was a slave) Robespierre tried to escape by jumping out of a window but only succeeded on landing on some bayonets and an unfortunate French peasant. He lived – albeit grievously injured - and was promptly jailed. He was condemned on 28 July – having not been allowed a defence – and transported to the guillotine as crowds jeered.

Augustin de Robespierre

Engraving "The Death of Robespierre", circa 1799

Having been the protégé of Robespierre's brother, Napoleon fell under suspicion and was himself arrested and imprisoned. As France started to calm once more, 'Citizen Bonaparte' was released in September 1794, having condemned the Robespierre's and their philosophy. However his association with the Robespierre name still blighted his career and he was not chosen to command the artillery used in the invasion of Italy. He was fortunate. Others were executed for their connections.

STARTING AFRESH

Napoleon's military career could have ended with his unfortunate connection to the Robespierres brothers but with his customary determination he picked himself up and started to make fresh connections. The war in Italy was going badly, and an exhausted and disorganised French government could do little more than mount a defence. It was Napoleon who got the ear of General Dumerbion, the army commander, and suggested a bold attacking strategy instead. It was against Dumerbion's every instinct, but somehow Napoleon persuaded him. On 21 September 1794, Dumerbion put Napoleon's plan into effect, catching and badly beating the Austrian army at Dego on the River Savona. Having won a major victory, it was Napoleon's instinct to advance deeper in Italy but this was just too much for Dumerbion, who refused and instead settled back in a strictly defensive position once more.

Napoleon received credit, but it was still not enough to rehabilitate his reputation. He promptly went to Paris, where he sought to win some political support and revitalise his career – but it didn't happen. He was still one of Robespierre's men. Indeed, Napoleon found himself posted to the infantry – and with a sizable pay cut. It was an effective demotion and Napoleon faked serious ill-health to avoid the new post. He was put on unpaid leave. Now Napoleon's resolve started to wear thin. He was unused to being treated in this way and gave very serious thought to leaving the French army and instead heading off to Turkey to offer his services to the Ottomans as a mercenary. Short of money and forced to sell some of his possessions, he even tried his hand at becoming a romantic novelist.

A BETTER CHOICE OF FRIENDS

Fortunately for Napoleon, he still had one connection to help him advance – and he was a man going places. The Vicomte Paul de Barras was a former royalist officer who had defected to the

Vicomte Paul de Barras

revolutionaries and then turned counter-revolutionary again to help end the Terror. With the French government – now called 'The Directory' - still in chaos and Royalist sentiment on the ascendancy, it had appointed Barras to the vital role of maintaining law and order. He thought Napoleon a good man, and appointed him as the second-in-command of the Troops of the Interior.

On 5 October 1795, an armed group of some 30,000 – most of them ex-soldiers - took to the streets of Paris once more, eager to bring down the government. As they advanced on the Tuileries Palace, which housed the government, Napoleon met them with 40 guns of his beloved artillery. They were lured into a wide open space where the guns could have most effect and then fired on with caseshot and grapeshot at near point blank range. Napoleon had chosen the ammunition deliberately. Once fired it spread out, killing fewer but maiming a great deal more. It was a deliberate terror weapon. The ground was littered with screaming casualties, blown-off limbs and pools of blood. The mob froze, then started to scramble away in fear. The entire engagement lasted just two hours and saw Napoleon have his horse shot dead from under him (the first of twenty during his career). Although he could not know it at the time, Napoleon had just fired the final shots of the French Revolution. He had warned Barras in advance that he intended to take stern action on the day, saying, *'Once my sword is drawn, it will not be sheathed until order is restored'*.

Having effectively saved the government, members were suddenly more kindly disposed to him. Napoleon was now made a full general and appointed commander of home forces, but that was not nearly enough for him. He wanted the position of head of the French Army in Italy – and he got it, just five months after saving the government. Napoleon did not suspect that the government were already nervous about having such an ambitious young man hanging around their capital.

Etchings, showing the failed assault in Paris on 5 October 1795

JOSEPHINE

'I awake full of you. Your image and the memory of last night's intoxicating pleasures has left no rest to my senses'

Napoleon

'You to whom nature has given spirit, sweetness, and beauty, you who alone can move and rule my heart, you who know all too well the absolute empire you exercise over it!'

Napoleon

'He does not love me, he worships me. I think he will go mad'

Josephine

'The only thing that ever came between us was my debts; certainly not his manhood.'

Josephine

The first time Napoleon met Josephine, he saw the woman of his dreams. The first time Josephine met Napoleon, she saw a meal ticket.

Josephine was not her real name. That was Napoleon's nickname for her. She had been born Marie Josèphe Rose Tascher de La Pagerie and as a child was called Yeyette. When the couple met she was calling herself Rose. Whatever she was called, she was attractive, sophisticated and self-possessed. Her hobbies included art, fashion, horticulture and spending her lovers' money, at which

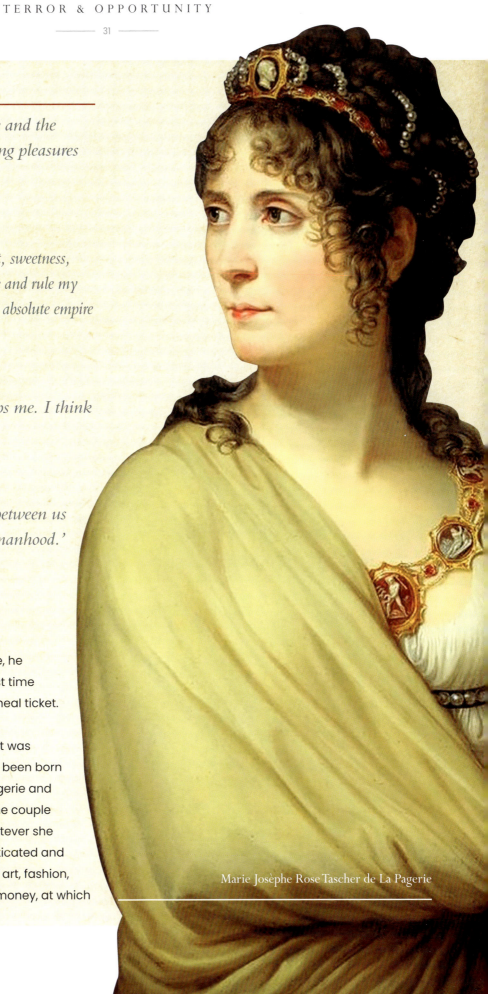

Marie Josèphe Rose Tascher de La Pagerie

Alexandre de Beauharnais

Coiffure à la guillotine

she proved particularly adept. Contemporaries describe her dark-haired and dark eyed, of average height and with a good figure and a clear complexion. She was not conventionally beautiful, but her personality could be mesmerising. Her only flaw was her rotting teeth. To hide them, she frequently spoke with her handkerchief over her mouth and learned to smile through closed lips.

The daughter of once-wealthy plantation owners on the Caribbean island of Mustique, who had been driven to near financial ruin by a series of devastating hurricanes, Josephine had been brought to France at the tender age of sixteen to be married off. She became the wife of a 19-year-old aristocrat and soldier, Alexandre de Beauharnais. The couple had two children but Alexandre preferred being in the brothel to staying at home and the couple separated. Alexandre dismissed her as 'a creature with whom

I can find nothing in common' and delighted in sending her hurtful and abusive letters. During the Terror, Alexandre had been arrested for doing too poor a job of defending the town of Mainz, imprisoned and then guillotined. Josephine only escaped the same fate because of the fall and execution of Robespierre. She fully expected to die and, in preparation, had already cropped her hair in a style bitterly called the *'coiffure à la guillotine'* by its forthcoming victims.

Widowed and with two children, Josephine survived the only way she knew, by becoming the mistress of powerful men. Her previous connections in society gave her access to some of the most important men in the nation and she slept her way through them until she ended up as the mistress of Paul Barras, who saw Napoleon as his protégé. They stayed together amid rumours of wild orgies until Barras decided he wanted someone a lot younger and schemed to dump Josephine on naive young Napoleon.

When they first met, she was six years older than he was, but nevertheless Napoleon happily took the bait. He had until this time only limited experience with women and Josephine simply overawed him. He desperately wanted a wife of high status which would assuage his ego, but he had been rebuffed on several occasions by women who thought he was beneath them. For her part, Josephine thought he was a short and dubious man with lank hair and a pale, unhealthy complexion. He was scruffy, utterly humourless, reeked of eau de cologne and his boots smelled bad. She was baffled why her ex-lover spoke so highly of him. Her opinion changed as he became more successful and powerful, but love was not a word she would have used to describe her feelings. *'What I feel is tepidness,'* she confessed to a friend.

The almost-penniless Josephine first became Napoleon's mistress and then his wife in March 1796 when she was thirty two. Perhaps possessed of more common sense than the smitten Napoleon, his family did not approve of their marriage. His mother made no secret of how much she disliked Josephine, thinking her far too stuck up and haughty. Furthermore she was too old for him and already had two children.

Two weeks after their civil wedding, conducted in a Parisian registry office, Napoleon set off to conquer Italy and Josephine slipped into bed with a dashing young Hussar.

Engraving, the Civil Marriage of Napoleon and Josephine

THE FIRST ITALIAN CAMPAIGN

'In our time, no one has the slightest conception of what is great. It is up to me to give them an example.'
Napoleon, 1796

Napoleon's new command of the army in Italy proved, at first at least – something of a poisoned chalice. France had declared war on virtually every country in Western Europe, but didn't have anything like the funds available to adequately pay for their military. When he arrived in Nice to take command, he was expecting to find over 100,000 men. In reality, he found less than 30,000. Thousands had deserted. They were not being paid and morale had plummeted. His beloved artillery was down to strength of just 60 guns. No new guns had been bought. Of France's ten armies, the army in Italy was undoubtedly in the worst shape and hardly fit to fight at all. There was a shortage of everything from guns to uniforms, bayonets to shoes, food to ammunition.

On 28 March 1796, he made a grand proclamation in a desperate attempt to raise morale:

'Soldiers, you are naked, ill fed…but rich provinces and great towns will soon be in your power!'

He promised them booty. They would live off the land while waging war and would plunder themselves rich. The troops responded positively. He also got them more food and back pay started to be issued. The common soldier's love affair with Napoleon started here.

The attack began in April with French forces in Northern Italy winning the first battles of the campaign at Montenotte and Mondovi, and knocking the forces of Piedmont out of the fight in just two weeks before their Austrian allies could even respond. France took 5,000 losses, but it's estimated that Piedmont lost 25,000 men. This was a new kind of war, conducted at lightning speed. In the 20th century, they would call it Blitzkrieg. It was also the divide and conquer

Napoleon Bonaparte and his staff during the Italian campaign in 1796

strategy that Napoleon would use time and again until Waterloo.

With Piedmont gone, Napoleon focused his forces against the Austrians – although he would also knock out the Sardinians in just five days for good measure, sending them scurrying back to Turin. Victories at Dego, Codogno and Lodi followed . On 13 May, French troops marched into Milan. In November, he won a crushing victory at Arcole after crossing the River Alpine. The three day battle at Arcole was won despite Napoleon having fewer troops. He cunningly convinced the Austrians that they were almost surrounded and they hastily withdrew. In January the following year he again beat the Austrians, this time at Rivoli, where the Austrian dead numbered something like 14,000 for 5,000 French losses. Austrian influence in Italy simply collapsed.

All this delighted the French public back home. Patriotic fervour revived and with it hero worship for the general who brought them honour and glory. Napoleon sensed this was important and set up his own newspaper back home in France as well as one for his troops. And so what if there should be a little spinning and the odd exaggeration?

Napoleon in Italy, 1796

Napoleon Bonaparte on the Bridge at Arcole
by Antoine-Jean Gros

Napoleon in fact brought them more than this, thanks to his shameless looting. Vast amounts of precious metals, jewels and works of art were sent back to Paris, some for himself and some for members of the Directory and the state treasury itself. They liked the new influx of riches and in consequence gave Napoleon more and more autonomy. They also sent him reinforcements, so that he now commanded an army some 50,000 strong.

Napoleon was careful not to totally alienate the Roman Catholic Church. He understood what a useful means of control they exerted over the population and fully intended to use them if he could. However, he was not above seizing their gold and silver finery and looking after it *'for safekeeping.'*

Once firmly in control of the region, Napoleon started to reshape its political landscape, to ensure long-term control. 'Patriot' Committees were established in every main town to exert authority on behalf of the French. New republican states were set up, over twenty of them, each with a new constitution drawn up by Napoleon himself. The rulers of venerable old Venice and Genoa were brought low and now he controlled them too. The grand idea was that he was bringing liberty, but in reality he was just enforcing control.

During the campaign, Napoleon never failed to write home to Josephine every day, expressing his ardour fulsomely. Her letters back were far less frequent and sometimes oddly prosaic. He kept her picture in his pocket wherever he went and delighted in showing it to others. She put his portrait in a drawer and forgot it.

Napoleon was just twenty-eight years old. He was a man undoubtedly going places. The government feared that place might be Paris next. They understood now just how ambitious he was, and desperately searched around for something else to keep him busy and away from the seat of power. In Rome, even the pope started uttering warnings about this new man Napoleon. There were rumblings that the man might just conceivably be the antichrist.

General Bonaparte on horseback and his staff reviewing a troop of Austrian prisoners

'EUROPE IS TOO SMALL FOR ME'; THE INVASION OF EGYPT

'Europe is too small for me…I must go East.'
Napoleon

'Europe is but a molehill - all the great reputations have come from Asia.'
Napoleon

'I was full of dreams. I saw myself founding a new religion, marching into Asia riding an elephant, a turban on my head, and in my hand the new Koran.'
Napoleon

When Napoleon wrapped up his campaign in Italy, back in Paris the Directory quite expected him to return in triumph at the head of his army like his great hero Caesar. He would then cross the Rubicon – or in this case the Seine – seize power and crown himself whatever he fancied crowning himself. It didn't happen. Instead, when he returned to the capital in December 1797, he was still oddly loyal. The Directory counted their blessings and started planning to send him off again on behalf of a grateful nation. Foreign Minister Talleyrand suggested that Napoleon should launch an invasion of Great Britain, but this was met with some scepticism. Napoleon knew that France did not have the ships or the funds to do a half-decent job of an invasion – and Napoleon didn't take at all to the idea of contesting the Channel with the most powerful navy in the entire world.

While the Directory were desperately trying to come up with another plan, Napoleon helpfully decided on one of his own. He would conquer Egypt. The land of the pharaohs held a strange enchantment over French society and such a campaign would also satisfy Napoleon's fantasy to be the next Alexander the Great, whom he regarded as even more magnificent than Caesar. He told the Directory that

Foreign Minister Talleyrand

his ultimate aims were to build a 'Suez Canal', easing access into the Indian Ocean and then link up with patriot forces on the Indian sub-continent and drive the British from their most valuable possession. At the same time, holding Egypt would give him a base from which to sweep up the Levant and conquer Turkey when the time came. He could, he told his masters, do it with just 30,000 French troops plus another 30,000 local mercenaries, 50,000 camels and 150 cannon. He calculated that he would need just four months to start menacing the British in India.

Secretly delighted (Egypt and India were much further away from Paris), the Directory agreed – provided Napoleon could finance the assault himself. Within weeks, Napoleon had raided the treasuries of the Vatican, the Swiss and the Dutch and come up with 10 million Francs to finance the assault.

When it sailed, Napoleon was just 29 and his fleet consisted of over 300 ships. His senior officers included Murat who liked wearing outrageously outré costumes and pink trousers into battle, Desaix who was hideously disfigured by a sabre slash, one-legged Caffarelli, Berthier, who kept a shrine dedicated to an Italian woman in his cabin complete with altar and candles and the soon to be '*dans la merde*' Kléber. Those on board included more than troops. Over 160 academics shipped out with him, and artists too. Napoleon had worked hard to create a public relations image for the assault that appealed to French self-satisfaction and smugness: He would lead

Napoleon and his General Staff in Egypt by Jean-Léon Gérôme

a grand civilising mission into a lost ancient kingdom, uncovering knowledge and treasure without measure and helping to restore the fallen land to greatness with French culture. On his way to Egypt, Napoleon couldn't resist seizing and looting Malta, overthrowing its authorities and imposing a new constitution.

On 2 July 1798, Napoleon landed at Alexandria and marched on the city. A number of his forces, including both men and women, were captured by marauding Bedouin tribesmen on the way. The men were raped, the women beaten up. This oddity was put down to the imbibing of camel milk. Napoleon seized Alexandria, promising his victorious troops plunder once more, plus land back home in France after they returned. He wasted no time in marching south on Cairo but unfortunately for his men chose to go through the desert rather than follow the Nile. The force soon ran out of water and Bedouins made sure to poison every well in their path. Some soldiers died of thirst. Others went out of their minds and killed themselves.

By the time they reached the Pyramids at Giza, Napoleon's entire army was close to mutiny. They were distracted from mutiny by battle. Egyptian cavalry was on the way to intercept them, and they formed up for battle in giant defensive squares almost within sight of the Pyramids. The much feared cavalry of the Mamluk rulers came out to meet them on 21 July – and were duly butchered by close-in superior French firepower. As the Mamluks rode around and around the French squares looking for a breach to exploit, the enemy muskets were so close that fire sprang from the guns and caught the riders' robes alight. Many were transformed in just seconds into mounted human torches. The battle was all over in an hour. It's thought that over 10,000 Egyptians died that day. France lost 29 men. From Giza, Napoleon progressed to nearby Cairo where he had himself declared both the ruler of Egypt and Protector of Islam, while also setting up a puppet government. It seemed as if Napoleon could do no wrong. And then everything went wrong.

Admiral Nelson and the Royal Navy destroyed virtually all of Napoleon's fleet left behind in Alexandria Harbour. They included the 120-gun flagship *L'Orient*, sunk when her powder stores exploded and taking one thousand of her crew with her, not to mention the bulk of Napoleon's treasury. Just four French ships

Admiral Nelson

General Bonaparte in Cairo by Jean-Léon Gérôme

The Battle of the Pyramids by François-Louis-Joseph Watteau

survived in what became known as the 'Battle of the Nile' and they fled for France, leaving Napoleon and his troops with no way home. Turkey declared war on France over the incursion. A mob from the bazaar killed 250 French troops including one of Napoleon's aides-de-camp (whose body was thrown to the dogs). Napoleon responded by killing over 2,000 Arab civilians. Bubonic plague broke out, killing another 3,000 of Napoleon's soldiery. Napoleon tried to have his name spoken in the same breath as the Prophet Mohammed, but failed. His Egyptian cronies called Napoleon ' *a worthy son of the Prophet*' and *'favourite of Allah.'* The Egyptians were not that gullible and waged an increasingly harsh guerrilla war on the French. An underground manifesto declared *'The French people are a nation of stubborn infidels and unbridled rascals... They look upon the Koran, the Old Testament and the New Testament as fables.'*

And perhaps worst of all, word reached Napoleon that Josephine was being unfaithful back home. He was beside himself, threatening a public humiliating divorce and to take out his anger on the French people themselves, threatening to *'exterminate that race of puppies and pretty boys!'* In sympathy, the Bey offered him the use of an eleven year old girl, but he didn't really enjoy her. Undeterred, the Bey then gave him a little boy, but that was no better.

Napoleon was now in the foulest of moods. He was used to winning. Now everything seemed to be collapsing around his ears. Eager to do something – anything – to save his reputation, he advanced east and north through Palestine to take Syria. Along the way, he took 4,500 prisoners – including women and children at Jaffa - then promptly had them all slaughtered by bayonet or else by drowning, lest they cause trouble. The butchery went on for three full days. Napoleon's forces had just solved the problem of what to do with their prisoners when they were hit by a second outbreak of bubonic plague. Napoleon made sure that his visit to his sick men in hospital was captured for all time by having an official artist draw the tender moment.

Now it was on to the ancient city of Acre – and Napoleon's first major defeat. The defenders of the city – Turks under the command of British admiral Sidney Smith – successfully fought him off. So comprehensive was the defeat that Napoleon decided to retreat back to Egypt. He now had just 8,000 men out of the 14,000 he had set out with to menace Syria. More died in a succession of huge sandstorms during the retreat through the Sinai Desert or from bombardments by British warships off the coast. Some simply starved to death, or killed themselves along the way. It's also believed that Napoleon had some of his sicker troops poisoned to death with opium so they would not slow down his retreat. It was a truly ragtag bunch of exhausted stragglers who returned to Cairo – but Napoleon deliberately staged their return to look like a grand victory parade.

Napoleon wanted out. However, if he just went it would appear that he had been an abject failure and he could say goodbye to his future. So instead, he cast about for an excuse. Back home, France was under threat from foreign neighbours again and, he said, it was obvious that the Directory couldn't handle it. They were cowards to a man. He dismissed them as *'that bunch of lawyers'* and, perhaps more harshly *'only fit to piss on'*. He, Napoleon, must return to France immediately and save the entire nation from ruination. Put like that, his high command could not help but agree. A week later, in August 1799, he was on a ship bound for France, leaving Jean-Baptiste Kléber in charge of what remained of his forces in Egypt. *'He has left us avec ses culottes plein de merde,'* he said bitterly, under no illusions as to why Napoleon suddenly disappeared. French forces finally surrendered in Egypt in September 1800 and the survivors were ferried home in British ships. Two years later, Egypt was formally returned to Turkey.

Admiral Sidney Smith

C3 SEIZING POWER

POWER AND A HAIRCUT

Napoleon glowered and fumed for every minute of his sea crossing back to France, then raced across the nation with such speed that he was in Paris before the Directory even found out he'd left Egypt. He was unsure how he would be greeted, as news might have leaked of his Egyptian debacle, but he found himself returning to a fulsome hero's welcome. Although the military threats that had plagued France during what became known as The War of the Second Coalition, had largely been solved now by other generals, the French population were beset with chronic inflation. Where once there was fifty francs to a gold franc, now there was 100,000 francs. There were food shortages too, mass unemployment and unpopular conscription laws. Everyone hated the Directory and more and more were looking to Napoleon to save the nation. Napoleon had picked the perfect time to come home. He sorted matters out with Josephine – somewhat noisily – and then turned to matters politic.

In November 1799, what became known as the 18 Brumaire Coup, Napoleon pulled together a political coalition which overthrew the Directory. To their credit, the members of the Directory's two chambers – the Elders and the Council of the 500 - did put up a fight, physically attacking Napoleon when he entered their chamber to disband them. He was only rescued by his military escort and was left bloody and shaken. There and then he denounced the Elders as *'in the pay of England'* and ordered their arrest. Politicians fled in all directions, some even diving through windows to escape, but they were all seized and arrested, the last to remain free being found hiding in the bushes outside the building. He justified his actions by saying,

'I believe it my duty to my fellow citizens, to the soldiers perishing in our armies, to the national glory bought with their blood to accept the command.'

Installation of the Council of State at the Palais du Petit-Luxembourg, December 25, 1799

British political cartoon Caricature of Napoleon, circa 1799

Napoleon Bonaparte in the coup d'état of 18 Brumaire

The drafting of a new constitution followed, which was ready by mid-December 1799 and voted for by a somewhat untrustworthy 3,011,007 citizens to 1,567 votes in January 1800. Napoleon's brother Lucien is widely believed to be behind the fraud. The Directory was done away with and a Consulate set up with Napoleon as First Consul, now on a salary of 500,000 Francs a year. The other two in the Triumvirate were selected by Napoleon himself and only had consultative powers. The parliamentary bodies he established were likewise just puppet shows. He now effectively controlled France, promising what the French desired most – peace, law, justice and order. Napoleon was still only 30 and – as a concession to the French people – he had his hair cut to look less ragged and more responsible. He also schemed just a little to win more Royalist support. He was now far more powerful than Louis XVI had ever dreamed of being. By 1802, Napoleon had elected himself Consul for Life, or rather a vote by the public did. It gave him 99.7% approval. It still wasn't enough for him.

Napoleon in the Battle of Marengo

THE SECOND ITALIAN CAMPAIGN

While Napoleon had been promoting French culture and civilisation in Egypt, the Austrians had reconquered Northern Italy and pretty much obliterated what Napoleon had created there. It was a personal affront he simply couldn't let pass.

In May 1800, Napoleon led an army of fully 50,000 men through the Great Saint Bernard Pass in the Alps and caught the Austrians by surprise. Although it was May, they still thought the pass unusable due to massive snowdrifts and treacherous ice. They were wrong. One of the most famous paintings of Napoleon shows him mounted on horseback, spurring his troops on. This is historically false, as in fact Napoleon traversed the pass on a mule, incessantly cursing it and slapping it for slipping and sliding everywhere. Most of the army made it, but much of their heavy equipment and supplies were lost. Back home the French people thrilled at Napoleon's daring: Where once he was Caesar and Alexander, now he was Hannibal.

The following Battle of Marengo on 14 June 1800 was claimed at the time to be a stunning victory for Napoleon, and is still widely remembered as

Napoleon Crossing the Alps by Jacques-Louis David

Painting depicting the signing of Treaty of Amiens, between France and Britain, signed by Napoleon and Cornwallis

General Desaix

such. In truth, he very nearly lost. He had a force of 24,000 with him, compared to the Austrian's 30,000 and was also chronically short of artillery pieces. The battle started with the French Army taken by surprise and consequently forced onto the retreat, despite Napoleon riding back and forth along his lines urging his men to stand fast and fight. By 3pm, things had gone so well for the Austrians that their commander considered it was all over and left the field, having delegated to his subordinates the task of mopping up. Only the arrival of General Desaix with a division of French cavalry at his back saved the day. The reinforcements had good artillery support and routed the Austrians in a series of devastating cavalry charges. The Austrians broke and fled across a river. They had lost some 14,000 men.

Within 24 hours, the Austrians surrendered and agreed to leave Italy once more. All their fortresses were surrendered to the French. Once out of Italy though, they became truculent once more and Napoleon was forced to send another army under General Moreau to deal with them, which he did very decisively at the Battle of Hohenlinden in December 1800. After that, the Austrians, temporarily at least, became much more compliant.

Back home, Napoleon quite naturally took all the credit. He basked in the glory of his reconquest of Italy and his reputation grew still higher.

SURVIVING THE PEACE

'I closed the gulf of anarchy and cleared the chaos.'
Napoleon

With the Austrians pacified, for now at least, and the British reaching a fragile agreement with the Treaty of Amiens in 1802, Napoleon found himself presiding over a rare moment of peace in France. His popularity grew to new heights. The economy was finally starting to improve and France enjoyed a reputation as one of the great powers once again.

With France in his pocket, Napoleon turned his attentions to the long neglected French empire. The Caribbean island of St Dominique used to be one of

Napoleon Bonaparte circa 1799

France's greatest sources of wealth, but short-sighted politicians had abolished human slavery in 1794, wrecking the profit. Napoleon swiftly reintroduced slavery in all the French Caribbean colonies and this decree remained in effect for another fifty years. In response, the people of St Dominique rose up to stay free. Napoleon sent two armies to crush them, but failed both times. The French quit – and the island state of Haiti was established.

Other reforms were more successful. He changed the tax system, brought down rate of interest on borrowing and managed to squeeze inflation out of the nation's economy. Access to government positions was made more meritocratic. He somewhat elevated the despised peasant class and worked towards the goal of universal education, fought to establish equality of all under the law, advanced freedom of religion and creating the Code Napoleon of civil law, which is still the basis of much law in Europe to this day. He gave further support to the arts and sciences. One part of his commitment to the arts was to ensure lots of paintings were made of him in heroic poses, which were then placed where the public could admire them properly. He set up the first successful French national bank. The 'French Washington' as he was now coming to be called in some circles smoothed things over somewhat with the Catholic Church.

During the period 1800 to 1804, Napoleon survived several assassination attempts. His murder of a Swiss-German nobleman vaguely implicated in a plot in 1804 stirred up international hostility against him. The assassination attempts focused Napoleon's mind somewhat. If he was to die, then what? His answer was to get the French people to vote him Emperor of the French - and they did, by a suspicious margin of some 99%. In fact just 2,569 Frenchmen voted against it. Just like a king, his first born would now assume the title when he died. For now though, Napoleon Bonaparte was Napoleon I – and what he really needed now was a son and heir.

THE THIRD COALITION

The fragile peace between Britain and France lasted barely a year. Britain reneged on its agreement to vacate Malta and the French failed to honour a promise to respect the Dutch. In fury, Napoleon lost his patience and summoned the British ambassador, Lord Whitworth. He proceeded to stand there and scream at the diplomat in a vain attempt to bully him. Since Whitworth towered above him in stature and kept his dignity throughout, he just looked silly. On a later occasion, Napoleon again had a screaming fit at Lord Whitworth and then strutted towards the door – only to find his servant unable to open it. He was forced to stand there looking stupid until his servants could free the door and let him out.

Britain - hardly surprisingly - had once again declared war on the French, though little had happened since. The British had postured and Napoleon had responded by stationing a large military presence on the Channel Coast. Napoleon had a particular dislike of Britain, a country he called *'the vampire of the north'*. Its people he famously reduced to *'that nation of shopkeepers'*. He hated the fact that it would take a sea campaign to get at them and that Britain used its trading wealth to sponsor anti-Napoleonic sentiment throughout Europe. At heart, he thought Britain was weak and undeserving of its influence and empire.

Behind the scenes though, Britain was pumping vast amounts of gold coins into France to support the enemies of Napoleon. On the international stage, Britain

British ambassador, Lord Whitworth

"The Political See-Saw / The Political Swing". Napoleon plays Swiss aristocrats and democrats against each other and annexes the canton of Valais

drew up agreements with first the Swedes and later the Russians, Austrians and Prussians to form yet another Coalition against Napoleon. Everyone recognised him as a military threat, but his more egalitarian domestic policies were also seen as threatening the old order. People in other countries were getting ideas...

THE POWER OF PROPAGANDA

"One must be a charlatan! That's the way to succeed."
Napoleon

'Four hostile newspapers are more to be feared than a thousand bayonets '
Napoleon

'It is not necessary to bury the truth. It is sufficient merely to delay it until nobody cares'
Napoleon

Napoleon had realised, as few military leaders had before him, the power of propaganda. Even by the time of his first Italian Campaign, he was taking time out to be sure to tell his side of events to the people back home as well as to his own troops, via the newspapers he owned. By the time he set off to conquer Egypt, what was in reality a bloody and inexcusable surge of conquest, it was portrayed as a French cultural achievement extraordinaire. When he looted Europe's art treasures, it was to stop pearls being spread before swine. France was the only place whose cultural heritage could possibly hope to appreciate them and display them to the world.

The Louvre had become the *Musee Napoleon*, in case anyone had any doubts who was behind this beneficence. He evoked French nationalism – and French cultural nationalism in particular – all the time, while in reality being a Corsican with no real love for France or the French. He appreciated the use of coarse nationalism though, to be sure. As a creation of the Revolution, he paid lip service to its ideals to win over the liberals and intelligencia of Europe. Most still believed in him long after they should have.

All over France, porcelain factories turned out commemorative plates and drinking vessels all bearing the image of Napoleon or members of his family. Limited edition casts were made of his sister Pauline's hand and foot. You could purchase busts of Napoleon or full length statues, either draped or undraped and even foreign artists were commissioned to celebrate the great man's physiogamy in statuary sometimes ten feet tall. Luxury commemorative vases depicted his victories or just his basic head. Now, the people could have Napoleon himself in their homes, and share in France's triumphs. It was all a bit Roman, but then that was how Napoleon thought and how he pictured the perfect state.

As he had become more powerful, even the newspapers which he didn't own became more willing to toe the line and present what he wanted to be presented. In 1800, 60 of the 73 Parisian newspapers were censored by decree. By 1811, only four remained. The theatres too, encouraged by his secret police, would stage only friendly works. Napoleon did not understand satire, let alone tolerate it.

He pretended to love his men, whereas in reality his ability to love did not extend all that very far from himself. He expected them to cheer him each time he turned up, and would tweak individual's noses or slap their faces while inspecting on the parade ground to suggest brotherhood. But he was not one of them. An average of 35,000 French troops died for every year of the Napoleonic Wars. He never showed concern, other than to widen conscription. Yet still they believed he cared about them, and this generated huge loyalty. The Duke of Wellington once estimated that Napoleon's presence on the battlefield was worth an extra 40,000 men. They died in their droves and in their ignorance.

'If you build an army of 100 lions and their leader is a dog, in any fight, the lions will die like a dog. But if you build an army of 100 dogs and their leader is a lion, all dogs will fight as a lion'
Napoleon

Early 19th century porcelain cabinet plates, with hand-painted portraits

Napoleon Bonaparte circa 1799

Laure Junot, Duchess of Abrantès

HAIL TO THE EMPEROR

'To be a king is to inherit old ideas and genealogy. I don't want to descend from anyone.'
Napoleon

'I am the successor, not of Louis XVI, but of Charlemagne'
Napoleon

'I have witnessed … the celebration of sumptuous and solemn festivals; but never did I see anything at all approximating in splendour to the coup d'oeil exhibited at Napoleon's coronation'
Laure Junot, Duchess of Abrantès

The imperial procession going to Notre-Dame for the coronation ceremony, December 2, 1804 Crossing the Pont-Neuf

Bonaparte practically ordered Pope Pius VIII himself to come to Paris and to officiate at his coronation as Emperor of the French. Predictably, Austrian cardinals advised him not to go whereas the Italian contingent was more positive. With his Genoan ancestry, they saw Napoleon as practically Italian and a good civilising influence on the ghastly French.

Napoleon was crowned emperor amidst the vast gothic splendour of Notre Dame Cathedral on Sunday 2 December 1804. The day before, he and Josephine had gone through an official religious marriage ceremony, as their first civil ceremony was not recognised by the Church.

On the day, the papal procession set out first, the pope escorted by 108 Dragoons. It was led by Nuncio Speroni, riding on a humble donkey and brandishing a large cross. History reports that there was no little sniggering from the crowd.

Napoleon on his Imperial Throne

Napoleon's carriage made for his coronation

Next came Napoleon's triumphant procession, setting out from the Tuileries to the cathedral. The soon-to-be emperor wore a costume drenched in satins and diamonds. He also wore high heels. The procession comprised 25 carriages and was escorted by no less than six regiments of French cavalry. 80,000 infantrymen were on standby in case trouble broke out. They arrived to find a huge hot air balloon tethered to the cathedral illuminated with over 3,000 lights and were greeted by a mass cry of 'Vive l'Empereur!' as they entered.

Before 20,000 guests the grand ceremony began – a unique and decidedly hokey mixture of old Catholicism, French nationalism and military pageantry. Napoleon's mother boycotted the ceremony. 300 musicians serenaded Napoleon and 400 choristers sang. In the end, Napoleon humiliated the Pope and took the crown himself from where it waited on the high altar before placing it on his own head, as if to recognise his own achievements. The crown was a modern fake, since the crown of Louis XVI had vanished during the Revolution. To make it seem important it was named *The Crown of Charlemagne*. He then proceeded to crown Josephine. Celebrations went on for a fortnight, costing some eight and a half million francs which the state of course paid for.

Coronation of Napoleon I

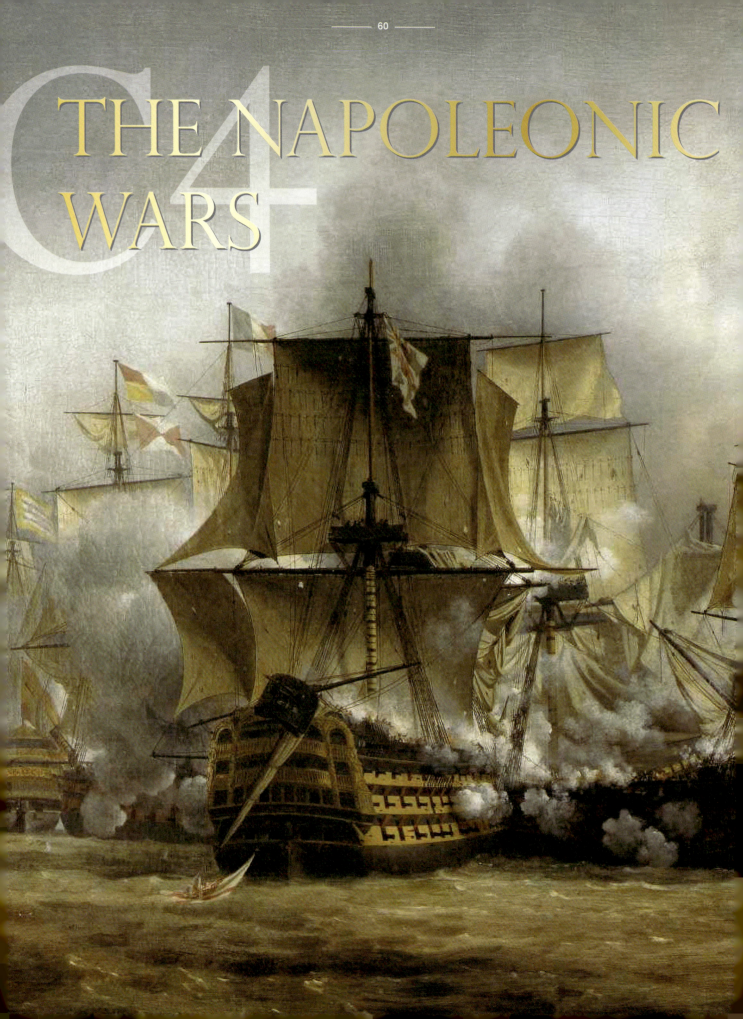

C4 THE NAPOLEONIC WARS

PREPARING FOR INVASION

'With God's help I will put an end to the future and very existence of England'
Napoleon

As Napoleon struggled with the logistics of invading Britain – and his fear of sea warfare - across the Channel most British people assumed he would be coming. The fires from his massive war camps of the Grand Army were clearly visible from England by night. There were claimed to be up to 200,000 French troops encamped there at the peak, and by day they practiced beach landings and invasion tactics. They were by and large Napoleon's best troops too, seasoned veterans. Rumours that Napoleon was on his way had English civilians steaming out of Dover and Folkestone on more than one occasion. Thousands rushed to join their local militias, but were often armed with little more than a pitchfork. By 1805, one in every five able bodied Englishmen was in uniform. New forts sprang up with alarming speed all along the Channel. Children were warned that Napoleon would slither down the chimney and seize them unless they were good. They called him *'Nappy'*. They called him *'Old Bony'*. They called him *'a mere insect, a pygmy'*. Cartoons showed him riding piggyback on the Devil. The British propaganda machine worked overtime to invent names and spread rumours; that London would be renamed Bonaparteopolis after the invasion, and British children would be deported to France. Britons would be mutilated in humiliating ways and then enslaved. No woman would be safe from rape. Rumours that Napoleon Bonaparte was the antichrist himself resurfaced. Cartoons abounded of John Bull hoisting aloft Napoleon's severed head on a pike.

Napoleon, 1806

LE DIABLE L'EMPORTE
SOUHAIT DE LA FRANCE.

warned him that the Royal Navy was far too strong for the invasion to commence. Furthermore, they pointed out, when the invasion barges had been tested in a large scale exercise, they proved ill-designed and many soldiers had drowned as a consequence. Napoleon pondered, and even considered taking his men across the Channel on hot air balloons, but this proved a pipe dream, as the prevailing winds were ill-suited. For their part, the over-paranoid British authorities believed that Napoleon might be building a secret channel tunnel or that he might come in French super ships powered by giant windmills.

Napoleon decided to try and lure the Royal Navy ships blocking the Channel away to the west. In early 1805, he sent a large combined French and Spanish fleet off to the West Indies to attack the British possessions there.

For his part, Napoleon dreamed of raiding the Bank of England and the British gold reserve to help fund future continental wars. Crushing Britain would also mean gaining access to her vast empire and all the further wealth it could provide him. He had lots of plans, as always, for a new administration. The Imperial Eagle would be planted on the Tower of London. King George would be overthrown and a republic established. With him would go the hated British aristocracy and the House of Lords. The nobility would forfeit all monies, and properties would be seized and (possibly) redistributed to the English poor. The French he would claim would come as friends to free the British in the name of Democracy. The English people were sure to rise up to support him...

2,000 flat bottomed invasion barges waited in the Channel ports but while Napoleon dreamed, his more pragmatic officers

King George III

He reasoned the Navy would have to go and confront them. They didn't. They stayed firmly on guard in the Channel. Napoleon's plan had failed. And then he got the shocking news that the old enemy, the Austrians, had declared war on France and were preparing to sweep through Bavaria and into France itself. Napoleon did not hesitate. He took by far the bulk of the Grand Army and headed east. The threat of invasion was lifted.

THE WAR OF THE THIRD COALITION

On 25 September 1805, Napoleon and his Grand Army from the Channel Coast reached the Rhine and began to surge across. Their target was the Austrian forces now occupying parts of the Southern German states. Napoleon was determined to knock them out quickly before they could receive Russian reinforcements.

General Karl Mack von Leiberich, in charge of the majority of Austrian forces stationed at the Fortress of Ulm, had barely time to realise what was going on before the French forces manoeuvred and effectively surrounded him. He was cut off and soon surrendered. The French took 60,000 prisoners in a single blow. Promised Russian reinforcements never arrived – the Austrians and the Russians used different calendars and there was much confusion about arrival dates. By November, Napoleon's men had crossed into Austria and seized Vienna. Then he waited for the Russians and the rest of the Austrian army to come out and fight him.

AUSTERLITZ – THE BATTLE OF THE THREE EMPERORS

'The battle of Austerlitz is the finest of all I have fought'
Napoleon

Napoleon had been using tricks against enemy forces for some time, trying to convince them that his army was far weaker than it really was and pretending to be putting out feelers for a peace deal. Meanwhile, sensing a historic victory, both the Russian Czar and the Austrian emperor turned up at Coalition high command eager to get involved and to dabble in strategy and tactics. It would be an unwise commander who told them no.

Austrian emperor, Francis I

Napoleon takes the surrender of General Mack and the Austrians at Ulm on October 20, 1805

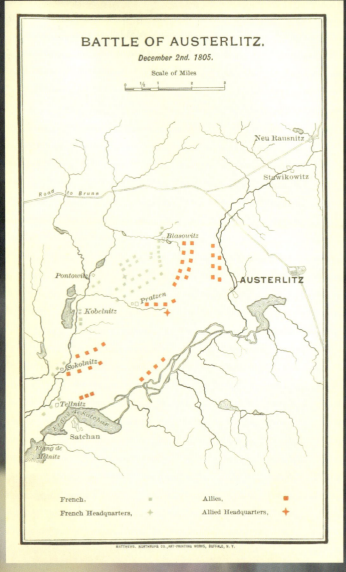

The Battle of Austerlitz took place in Moravia on 2 December 1805 with snow and ice on the ground and freezing fog blanketing the field of conflict. The Russian-Austrian forces numbered around 90,000 men and 280 cannon. The French fielded 73,000 men and 139 guns. As the opposing forces lined up at Austerlitz, Napoleon deliberately left an observable weakness in his right flank – and the Coalition fell into the trap. Almost as soon as battle commenced at 8am, they over-committed their forces to Napoleon's right flank, leaving their centre exposed. Napoleon then hit their centre hard, and it crumbled. After that, it was just a question of mopping up the flanks. The French suffered 9,000 casualties, their enemies 27,000 killed, wounded or captured.

It was all over for the Third Coalition. Austria conceded defeat immediately, and Napoleon punished them by seizing a number of their territories and 'fining' them 40 million francs. The surviving Russian soldiers were allowed safe passage to walk home.

Napoleon acknowledged his triumph by adopting all the children of the French troops who had died at Austerlitz, and announcing to his men, *'Soldiers! I am content with you.'*

The Battle of Austerlitz

TRAFALGAR

'No captain can do very wrong if he places his ship alongside that of the enemy.'
Vice Admiral Horatio Nelson

'England expects that every man will do his duty' – Flag signal from Admiral Nelson, 11.45am on the day of Trafalgar (The message was originally meant to have been 'England confides...' but they didn't have the right flags on board)

After its failed decoy mission to the Caribbean, Admiral Pierre Villeneuve's combined French and Spanish fleet of 33 warships returned to Europe. They were spotted at anchor in Cadiz Harbour. When their commanding officers heard that a British fleet under Vice Admiral Nelson was on the way to tackle them they held a vote – and decided not to come out to confront them as they sat 40 miles off Cadiz. At 27 ships, the Royal Navy fleet was smaller, but Villeneuve was nervous of Nelson after having sustained a resounding defeat at the Battle of the Nile.

On paper, the French enjoyed superiority in terms of individual ships. One had 136 guns - the *Santissima Trinidad*, the largest ship in the world.; two others had 112 guns each, whereas Nelson's elderly flagship *HMS Victory*, only boasted 100. When compared, the enemy fleet had almost 600 more cannon than the British.

Vice Admiral Horatio Nelson and 1805 Battle of Trafalgar Medal

However, the French crews were largely inexperienced – especially the gunners – and many of the French Navy's finest officers had been executed during the Revolution and Terror. The vote to stay safely in port was swiftly overturned by Napoleon himself, who told them in no uncertain terms to get out and fight.

The opposing fleets sighted each other at first light on 21 October 1805. Just eleven miles separated them but since the warships moved at just a fast walking pace, even in full sail, it took some hours for them to close. The first shots were fired at 11.50 am.

To overcome the enemy fleet's advantage in numbers of ships and guns, Nelson sailed his two columns of ships straight headlong at the French-Spanish line. The plan, which he called *'The Nelson Touch'*, was unorthodox and risky but in the event it worked and managed to shatter their traditional battle formation into three segments. The battle which followed last five full hours.

Nelson was shot by a French sniper on the deck of the Victory and died of his wounds just before the battle ended. His body was brought back in a rum barrel at first to Gibraltar and then to England for a state funeral. Villeneuve was captured and taken back to England where he later had the good manners to attend Nelson's funeral at St. Paul's Cathedral.

The combined Franco-Spanish fleet lost 22 ships in the fight. 11 further warships escaped back to port, but of those only five remained able to fight. The Royal Navy lost no ships, but they had 1500 men killed or wounded. Enemy casualties numbered some 7,000, with a further 20,000 captured. Many more sailors were deafened for life by the cannon fire. It was as decisive a victory as there could be, and French naval power was shattered. Napoleon committed his nation to an intensive shipbuilding programme but he never regained the strength he needed. There was no possibility of invading England now.

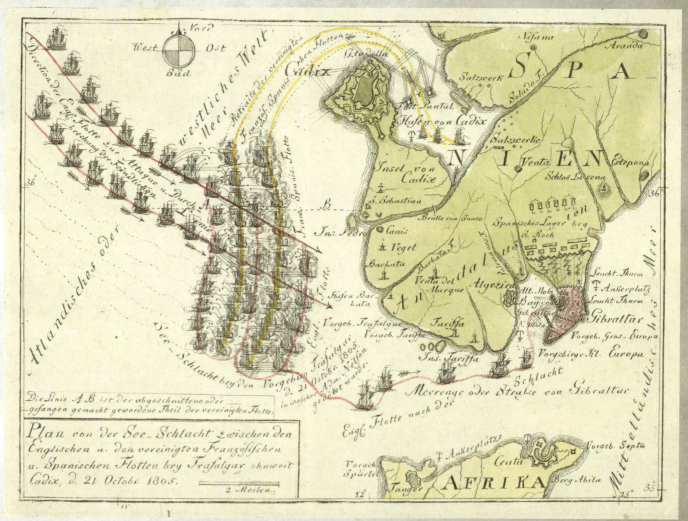

English advances formed in two closed groups against the Franco-Spanish fleet during the battle of Trafalgar

The Redoutable at Trafalgar

THE CONTINENTAL SYSTEM

Britain was not only master of the sea lanes but also the global leader in trade, bringing it continuous and exceptional wealth with which Napoleon and France simply could not compete. Napoleon's answer was to try and get all European nations to embargo trade with Britain. British goods would simply be banned and all communications severed, including mail services. The policy was announced in Berlin on 21 November 1806. Napoleon took it absolutely seriously and it became a key policy – one that he was willing to go to war to defend. Others did not share his view. Some creative approaches were taken to decide what was 'trade' and what wasn't, while some nations only applied the ruling sporadically. Some countries who adhered to Napoleon's decree actually became financially stricken as a result and one or two were almost bankrupted. Smugglers made a fortune running illicit British goods into continental Europe. The effect on Britain was minimal. Banned from Europe, the nation simply stepped up trade with the Americas and other parts of the globe.

Napoleon at the battle of Jena

THE FOURTH COALITION

Napoleon lost no time in setting up what became known as the Confederation of the Rhine, basically bringing together a number of German states but under French control. This quite understandably upset the Prussians, who were used to dominating much of Germany and in the summer of 1806, they decided to declare war on the French to win back their regional dominance.

French troops presenting the captured Prussian standards to Napoleon after the battle of Jena

THE NAPOLEONIC WARS

Napoleon went straight on the offensive. He marched 180,000 troops forward and hit the Prussians hard at the battles of Jena and Auerstedt, both fought on 15 October 1806. The blows struck were so vicious that control of the entire Prussian armed forces began to fall apart. As they retreated, the French rounded up 140,000 prisoners and captured thousands of cannon. Berlin fell. Angry at Prussia's defiance, he exacted a hard price for peace, taking a chunk of the nation for himself (and making his brother Jérôme king of the new land).

The threat from the Prussians ended, Napoleon marched east next to tackle Russian forces who had surged west into Poland. He was less successful this time. Two major battles in 1807 - Eylau and Heilsberg - ended in bloody stalemate. In June 1807, however, he finally achieved a decisive victory at the Battle of Friedland, and the Russians quickly sued for peace. Napoleon was much more lenient with the Russians than he had been with the Prussians, seizing some obscure islands, demanding their forces be removed from two areas – and insisting that Russia join the Continental System. There was little doubt now that the Emperor was dreaming of a united Europe, with himself as its head.

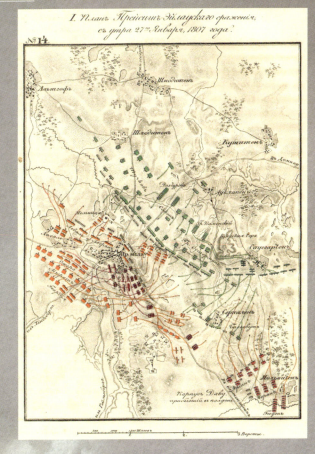

Map of The Battle Of Eylau

Medals from the battles of Jena & Eylau

Battle of Eylau 1807 by Jean-Antoine-Siméon Fort

Napoleon accepts the surrender of Madrid, 4 December 1808

PORTUGAL

Portugal had been constantly trading with the British, in defiance of the Continental system. Napoleon found this unforgiveable. With the connivance of the Spanish king, 24,000 French troops under Junot marched south over the Pyrenees in November 1807 and down through Spain. The Portuguese offered next to no resistance as Napoleon's forces pivoted into their nation and swept into Lisbon. They discovered that much of the Portuguese nobility had fled to Brazil and Junot wasted no time in disbanding the Portuguese army. With their leaders gone and their army finished, it was left to the ordinary people of Portugal to come together and start their own resistance movement. It was effective. The French never achieved any real control of territory outside of the capital.

…AND SPAIN

'With my banner bearing the words 'Liberty and Emancipation from Superstition', I shall be regarded as the liberator of Spain.'

Napoleon

Despite the fact that Spain was an ally, had sacrificed much of its fleet in the service of the French at Trafalgar, and given French armies complete freedom to march through their territory to get to Portugal, Napoleon decided he wanted to invade it.

French secret agents set to work stirring up rivalry between factions of the Spanish nobility, and by February 18 1808, Napoleon declared himself so alarmed by Spain's internal problems that he needed to become personally involved to help the poor benighted Spanish people. (whom he thought closer to inferior North Africans than true Europeans). This meant marching 120,000 troops down into Spain pretending at first to be allies on their way to Portugal. Spanish commanders simply didn't know how to react until the vast French force turned hostile and seized Madrid in March 1808. The monarchy was slung aside and Napoleon appointed his brother Joseph as the new King of Spain.

As with Portugal, while the nobility simply stayed out of the way, the ordinary people reacted violently to the French invasion and there were wild riots in Madrid just after the French seized the capital. Order was only restored with the use of bayonets by 20,000 French troops and hordes of vicious Egyptian Mamluk cavalry. Hundreds of civilians were rounded up and shot in the aftermath. 150 French soldiers died in the riots. Muslims were now killing Catholics once more in Spain which outraged the populace. Moreover, a new king that was not Catholic insulted their religious sensibilities and Napoleon was known to be unsympathetic to Catholicism. It became in part not just a patriotic uprising but a religious one too. The uprisings spread until they were almost commonplace throughout Spain. Other towns and cities rose up, waging guerrilla war against their occupiers. Parts of Portugal rose up too, only to be quelled by brutal massacres. In panic, the French rushed more troops to Spain. They had correctly anticipated that Spain's rulers were weak, but its people were another matter entirely.

French occupation troops found themselves critically short of supplies. Napoleon refused to send them more, saying they were an occupying army and could just take what they wanted from the people. This led to a

Joseph Bonaparte

succession of shocking massacres of farmers and peasants as well as mass rape. Spanish guerrillas responded by seizing any French soldier they could, cutting off his genitals and then burning him alive. Collaborators were murdered by the Spanish resistance.

At the same time, Spanish military resistance became more resolved – and successful. The Spanish Army of Andalusia defeated a French army at Bailén in July 1808. The French troops who took part were far from at their best. Food was short, 600 men got sick after drinking poisonous water and peasants regularly infiltrated the camp perimeters by night to loot and murder. The French also found it difficult to manoeuvre, weighted down as they were the sheer number of looted treasure wagons they had amassed while on campaign. Because of the multitude of troops that Napoleon had lost throughout Europe, many of the French soldiers were now young conscripts and no physical match for their Spanish enemies when it came to battle.

'But it was easy to perceive how astonished (the Spanish troops) were at the sight of our young infantry soldiers. The moral effect was wholly to our disadvantage, and as I compared the broad chests and powerful limbs of the Spaniards who surrounded us with those of our weak and weedy privates, my national pride was humbled.'

Baron de Marbot, a French Officer.

After a messy battle, the French surrendered. 17,000 soldiers were taken prisoner at Bailen. Most of them would never see France again, destined to starve to death as prisoners. France's reaction was to flee back North of the Ebro and abandon much of southern Spain to the rebels.

WELLINGTON IN PORTUGAL

Portugal had been one of Britain's closest allies for hundreds of years. When it was seized by the French, the British government simply found the situation intolerable. In August 1808, some 15,000 British troops invaded Portugal under the command of Lieutenant-General Sir Arthur Wellesley – later to be better known as the Duke of Wellington. Almost immediately, they began a march on Lisbon. They

Baron de Marbot

first defeated an army of 4,000 occupying French troops at Roliça, with the help of Portuguese troops who had previously been stood down. In short order, the Anglo-Portuguese force then met and smashed a French Army of some 14,000 men at Vimeiro. Britain had now effectively liberated Portugal from the French and were poised to move into Spain. There were some 30,000 British troops waiting in Portugal by mid-October 1808 under the new command of Sir John Moore and another 12,000 on the way from Falmouth.

NAPOLEON SAVES THE DAY

Napoleon was beside himself with anger when the news reached him. He raged that his army in Spain had been *commanded by postal inspectors rather than generals*. The commanding officers responsible

Sir John Moore

Battle Of Bailén

were court-marshalled, publically disgraced and imprisoned. (In 1812 Napoleon made the offense of surrendering to the enemy punishable by death). He would have to go to Spain and sort everything out himself. Gathering up the Grand Army once more, Napoleon marched south and proved much more successful than his officers in routing the Spanish and seizing back the territory he had lost.

It was an unfortunate time for Sir John Moore at the head of his relatively small Anglo-Portuguese army to decide to invade Spain. In short order, he was forced to retreat by Napoleon. The retreat became chaotic, there were a number of desperate rear-guard actions fought and the proposed invasion of Spain ended with Sir John Moore dead in battle and the remains of the British forces being evacuated by ship. British casualties during the campaign numbered some 7,000.

Napoleon couldn't stay to consolidate his victory though. The old enemy – the Austrians – were stirring once again. As he was prone to do, he announced that the problem in Spain had been solved by his magnificence and that he had to return to Paris on urgent business. In reality, the war would rage on for another six years – but at least he was out of it.

THE FIFTH COALITION

While Napoleon strove to avoid getting mired in the confusing war now being waged in Spain, Austria was positively excited to see the supposedly invincible French being defeated on the battlefield and struggling to cope against rag-tag peasant armies in Spain. Better news still, the French had to withdraw over 100,000 men from their German territories to reinforce their Spanish efforts. They determined it was now time to avenge all of their previous defeats. Allies were short on the ground this time, and Prussian promises of support came to nothing, but keeping its regular army mobilised was costing Austria huge sums of money and – if they didn't use it soon – the costs would be unsustainable.

The Battle of Aspern-Essling by Fernand Cormon

Napoleon at the Battle of Wagram

On 10 April 1809, Austrian troops crossed the Inn River to Invade French-run Bavaria. Within a week Napoleon had arrived in the area to take personal charge and with his characteristic aggression adopted a rapid offensive strategy which culminated in a victory at the Battle of Eckmühl later that month. He then marched into Vienna yet again but – having learned a thing or two from the Spanish – this time the Austrians did not automatically sue for peace.

A week later, the French tried to cross the Danube, and became embroiled in the Battle of Aspern-Essling. The sheer power of the sustained Austrian artillery bombardment forced Napoleon to retreat. Each side suffered around 23,000 casualties and Europe reeled at the news that Napoleon had suffered yet another defeat. Napoleon took more care with his battle plans to cross the Danube for a second time and it wasn't until early July 1809 that the crossing was made. 180,000 French troops took part. 150,000 Austrians were ready for them. The opposing armies met at the Battle of Wagram. It was the largest battle that Napoleon had fought in his career to date. He won, inflicting over 40,000 casualties on the Austrians and now convincing them to ask for peace terms. The terms Napoleon demanded – and got – were exacting, seizing considerable amounts of territory from the Austrian state.

At the end of July 1809, a British force of some 40,000 men landed in Holland to open up a second front against France, only to find that Austria had already surrendered. Following confusion over co-ordinating different forces, The British withdrew by December, but not before losing thousands of men to malaria.

'Lord Chatham with his sword drawn
Was waiting for Sir Richard Strachan.

Sir Richard, longing to be at 'em
Was waiting for the Earl of Chatham.'
Satirical English verse

French Imperial Guard charging Austrian dragoons at the Battle of Wagram

TROUBLE AT HOME

Napoleon and Josephine can hardly be considered as one of the world's most romantic couples. She more than had the measure of him from the start and no tactics he could dream up could overcome her need to cheat on him and spend as much of his money as she possibly could. He was far more enamoured of her than she was of him, and he would very likely have preferred a monogamous relationship with her, but he just couldn't make it happen.

To her, Napoleon was still a rough and unattractive little man of five foot five with smelly boots and feminine hands who wasn't getting any more appealing as he got older. She complained that he was an utterly selfish lover who was totally disinterested in her pleasure. He was also rather quick to be done. Still, the money was good and he had made her Empress.

It didn't take Napoleon long to become disenchanted. Josephine had started to cheat on him even before the ink on their marriage certificate was dry and her indelicacies while he was in Egypt were common knowledge amongst anyone who mattered. Napoleon took to cheating early too. He took many sexual partners while on campaign, telling his attendants when the urge came to *'bring me a woman'*. They duly did, naked so as to be sure she had no weapons on her. He cheated when back home too, even in the royal palaces, where Josephine was shut out of her own apartments until Napoleon had finished his rapid rutting.

After a while, the couple reached an odd compromise where Napoleon would tell his wife about some of his conquests, being sure to criticise their failings in looks or sexual prowess. When they rowed, it was more often than not over the bills Josephine had casually run up at Paris's leading fashion houses. Napoleon by nature was parsimonious and her greed baffled him. Nothing Napoleon said to her had any effect. Still, he remained fond of her, calling her his 'big beast' and getting her to read to him at night when he was home from campaign.

Since declaring himself Emperor, Napoleon had given more and more thought to building a dynasty based on inheritance and destined to be the greatest the world had ever known. There was just one problem – neither Napoleon nor Josephine were getting any younger – and they had yet to have children.

Grand Duchess Anna Pavlovna

NEW BEDFELLOWS

'It is a womb that I am marrying'
Napoleon

'In France women are considered too highly. They should not be regarded as on equality with men…they are nothing more than machines for producing children'
Napoleon

Marie-Louise of Austria

So Napoleon divorced Josephine on 10 January 1810 and started looking round for a younger woman to bear his heir. This woman would, however, have to come from the very best royal stock. There would be no more Creole women with bad teeth and a hankering for young cavalrymen. His eyes first fell upon the Czar of Russia's sisters. He first asked for the hand of Ekaterina and when that failed pursued her younger sister the Grand Duchess Anna Pavlovna. Napoleon considered Czar Alexander a friend now, and was personally hurt when the Czar moved to block any such relationship. It was obvious that he considered a Bonaparte far too lowborn to even look at his family. Seething with hurt, Napoleon would later invade Russia.

Napoleon looked around again and, ironically, his gaze fell upon blonde and buxom (but not bright) Princess Marie-Louise of his old arch-enemies the Habsburgs in Austria. They liked the idea of linking their family's future to Emperor Napoleon and little obstacles – Like Marie-Louise being half Napoleon's age and believing he was the Antichrist – were soon swept away. The couple were married in Paris on 1 April 1810 and elaborate decorations filled the city, much of it made of flimsy cardboard. The venue for the wedding ceremony was the Louvre. 8,000 guests lined the galleries to applaud the couple's progress through cheap cardboard facades on a Roman theme. As she walked, Marie-Louise noticed several paintings that had been looted from the Austrian palaces over the years. Thirteen cardinals refused to officiate at the ceremony, so Napoleon had them thrown out of their apartments and got his own uncle to do the job instead.

In March 1811 a child was born, Napoleon's son and heir (also named Napoleon), and placed in the most luxurious cradle in all of Europe. He was declared Napoleon II and The King of Rome. Marie Louise grew to like Napoleon. In consequence, it was four years before she started cheating on him.

Emperor Napoleon by Jean-Baptiste Isabey 1810

THE PENINSULAR WAR

When he did refer to it, Napoleon referred to the ongoing situation in Spain as *'the Spanish Ulcer.'* While Napoleon continued to regard Spain as a side issue – probably because he had no solution and knew that it was harming his image on the European stage.

After the British had been run off back to sea, French forces then retook Portugal in March 1809, under the command of Marshal Soult. They in turn were ejected again by a fresh wave of landed British troops now back under the command of Wellesley once more. By mid-1809, British forces were surging across the border into Spain as they had planned to do the previous year, with the French retreating before them. Remnants of the Spanish Army joined them. The Battle of Talavera on 27-28 July saw Wellesley achieve a significant defeat over the French and he was awarded with the new title of Viscount Wellington.

Threats of heavy French reinforcements brought the Anglo-Spanish force up short, and Wellington thought it advisable to retreat back in Portugal once more. Left to their own devices, the remaining Spanish forces advanced on Madrid but were soundly defeated. A further military defeat saw the surviving Spanish troops fleeing into the mountains of southern Spain to hide and to wage sporadic guerrilla warfare.

Meanwhile Wellington's forces back in Portugal prepared series of lines of formidable mountain defences – known as the Lines of Torres Vedras – to protect Lisbon in case the French returned yet again. The lines could communicate instantly with one another using semaphore. In front of the lines the British initiated a scorched earth policy, destroying crops and buildings so that any French force would have neither food nor shelter.

The French did return, in mid-1810 with a conquering army some 65,000 strong, under Marshal Maasena. Wellington inflicted heavy losses on the attacking French before being forced back inside his own well-prepared defensive lines. The French fell on the lines and were held. They too dug in, until Wellington's Scorched Earth policy really began to have an effect on them. The French Army were practically starving before they were ordered to pull back.

Marshal André Masséna

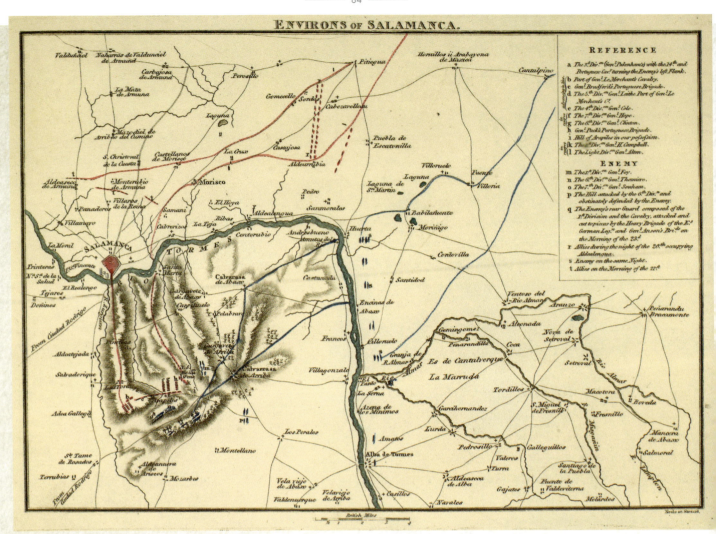

Map of Area surrounding Salamanca, showing disposition of troops before and after battle

In March 1811, Wellington went on the offensive from Portugal once more. This time, it was the turn of the Anglo-Portuguese and Anglo-Spanish forces to start besieging French garrisons, but with only mixed success. The war raged back and forth between 1811 and 1812, with neither side able to strike a knockout blow.

By now, the French were beginning to become more and more thinly stretched across the whole arena of battle. Facing determined guerrilla resistance, the French were compelled to use more and more of their troop strength to guard their long supply lines and consequently had fewer troops to use offensively. Finally, on 12 July 1812, a combined Anglo-Portuguese forced did manage to win a convincing victory over the French at Salamanca and, on 14 August, Madrid was liberated from the French. Napoleon's brother, the new king, fled. Throughout autumn, the combined forces advanced and the French retreated, trying to consolidate their position to push back. Eventually they rallied, counter-attacked and pushed Wellington all the way back into Portugal again. To achieve this, however, the French had to abandon a number of territories in order to muster sufficient focused manpower.

THE MARCH ON RUSSIA

'I have come once and for all to finish off these barbarians of the North.'
Napoleon

Spain was causing Napoleon more concerns than dead soldiers and dwindling resources. The seemingly intractable conflict was damaging his much-cherished reputation as Europe's invincible strongman. That was intolerable. He would, he thought, have to prove himself to both domestic and foreign doubters all over again.

He chose Russia. Opposition to Napoleon marrying his sisters by Czar Alexander had not been forgotten. Far from it. Napoleon seethed. There was also the matter of Russia not properly implementing Napoleon's Continental System and boycotting trade with Britain as they were obliged to do by treaty. War it would be. His advisors told him not to do it, but Napoleon overruled them.

Napoleon started to assemble a conquering army of truly gargantuan size, from the very start of 1812. When it was complete, it numbered some 650,000 men (although he boasted it was 800,000 strong). A third of the troops were French and the rest conscripted from conquered states including those in Germany, Italy, Hungary and Poland. The commanding officers were virtually all French. As it surged over the River Niemen in June 1812 and advanced into Russia, the invasion force stretched as long as 62 miles east to west. Behind the troops came the supporting baggage train. This in itself was over 6 miles long. It consisted of ammunition wagons, substitute horses, empty carriages for hauling away all the anticipated

Napoleon Before The Battle Of Moscow By Joseph Franque

plunder, grand carriages for the officers, 35,000 assorted wagons, drovers herding entire herds of cattle to be consumed en route, 950 cannon and over 30 million litres of wines and brandies. Standing watching this staggering procession from the roadside, it would have taken eight full days for the entire procession to pass. Napoleon had never commanded a force so mighty and it looked to all the world that it would fall upon Russia and crush it.

Napoleon had always considered Russia a cold land, and did not anticipate the fierce heat over its plains in high summer. He also did not know that the plains contained very little water and what there was of it was often brackish and filled with disease. By the beginning of autumn, diseases such as dysentery and typhoid had reduced his assault force by fully one half. The sun alternated with violent thunderstorms, turning the already poor quality roads into seas of mud. Wagons became stuck fast. Soldiers lost their boots to the sucking mud and had to march in bare feet. When the sun returned, it would bake the mud until it became like concrete, wedging wagon wheels in place. Food too was getting scarce and, ahead of him, Russian peasants were already adopting a 'Scorched Earth' policy, destroying any food sources and burning their own crops rather than leaving them to be captured by Napoleon. Meanwhile, the same peasants also adopted the Spanish tactic of kidnapping any stragglers from the column and burning them alive. The vast army started killing off its own horses to eat. Eyewitnesses described troops dragging down and eating horses before they could even be slaughtered and there were strong rumours of cannibalism too. It is little wonder then that more and more troops began to slip away and simply head home. Others killed themselves rather than continue.

BORODINO

'The most terrible of all my battles was the one before Moscow. The French showed themselves to be worthy of victory, but the Russians showed themselves worthy of being invincible'
Napoleon

Napoleon's plan had always been to lure the Russian army into one grand scale battle, defeat it and then march on Moscow to force the Czar to come to terms.

Battle of Borodino

In early September, it looked like he would have his wish, when 70,000 Russian infantrymen, supported by 25,000 cavalry and 600 cannon met Napoleon's army of some 160,000 men and 550 guns at the little village of Borodino 80 miles from Moscow. The battle lasted for three days, from 5 to 7 September, and Napoleon was shocked at how well his opponents performed. He had always thought the Russians (who were after all Slavs) mere rabble. Technically, Napoleon won the battle and the Russians withdrew but Napoleon took tremendous losses – some 50,000 compared with Russia's 40,000 - and the French cannon had been forced to use up much of their ammunition. At the height of the battle, opposing armies had been firing three cannons a second at each other.

MOSCOW

With Russian forces now withdrawn, Napoleon marched on to Moscow. In anticipation of his arrival, 270,000 Muscovites were evacuated and, a day after Napoleon arrived on 14 September, the Russians torched the city. Almost three quarters of the city's buildings were consumed in the flames, leaving little shelter for the invaders. Napoleon himself watched Moscow burn, recalling later

"Mountains of red, rolling flames like immense waves of the sea. Oh, it was the most grand, the most sublime, and the most terrifying sight the world ever beheld.'

There was precious little food to be pillaged in the city, and the French were once again forced to slaughter more of their horses to eat.

Napoleon had the capital now, and could simply wait for the Czar to surrender. That was the way Napoleon understood things, and the way such things were always settled. Only the Czar wouldn't reply to him. Napoleon sent a personal letter. No reply. He sent two delegations to conduct talk of terms. There was no interest shown by the Russians. And every day it was getting colder.

Napoleon suddenly realized his predicament. His men were freezing in a burned out city with precious little shelter, desperately short of food and about to be completely snowed in until spring. His men had no winter clothes. It felt for all the world like a trap. By 19 October, Napoleon reluctantly marched what was left of his men back out to Smolensk. Progress was slow.

Artwork depicting Moscow on fire

THE NAPOLEONIC WARS

Napoleon after The Battle Of Moscow

Map of Moscow showing the fire damage, in dark shade

They had after all eaten most of their horses. And all the while Russian forces counter-attacked the rear of their column. Napoleon succeeded in getting his troops to Smolensk by 9 November, only to find there was precious little to eat there either. He left four days later, at the head of a once-invincible army now no more than 40,000 strong. Much of the loot they had pillaged from Moscow had to be dumped along the way. He then lost a full half of his remaining strength struggling across the Berezina River at the end of the month. Everything was coming apart around him.

IMPERIAL BUSINESS!

Napoleon recognised that his grand Russian adventure had collapsed and he did what he tended to do in such a situation – he ran for home, leaving his officers and men to survive as best they could. Come 5 December, he announced to his commanding officers that there was urgent imperial business to attend to in Paris and he simply must go home. Leaving Marshal Murat with the unenviable task of assuming command, Napoleon fled west in a succession of horse-drawn sleighs, pulling rank and stealing the protective furs of his companions when the minus 25 degree temperatures really started to bite. His fur-less companions bitterly recalled later that he had spent much of the journey thinking up excuses and somehow blaming the British for what had befallen him. He eventually reached the relative warmth and safety of Warsaw, gave his excuses in a very repetitive – if not totally convincing – three hour speech and then continued west across Germany by sledge. By 18 December, he was home at his palace in Paris. His army were not so fortunate, struggling to get home through killing cold temperatures of -36f, snow blizzards, and all the whiles starving. Stories emerged of soldiers killing the few precious remaining horses, slitting them open and crawling inside for warmth. Along the way, 20,000 wounded soldiers were simply abandoned to their fate.

'The cold was so intense. One constantly found men who, overcome by the cold, had been forced to drop out and had fallen to the ground, too weak or too numb to stand...The road was covered with their corpses.' - Armand de Caulaincourt, advisor to Napoleon.

Of the 200,000 soldiers taken prison by the Russians, few survived to return home. Most died after just a

Napoleon leaves Moscow, the Kremlin in flames behind him

General von Blücher and Cossacks in Bautzen, 1813

few weeks in captivity. The Russian military did not press the fleeing French but the Peasants as well as roving Cossack bands continued to pick them off and kill them at every opportunity. Marshal Ney in charge of the rear-guard saw to it that the very last man that could be saved was out of Russia by 14 December. As many as 380,000 men under Napoleon's command are thought to have perished during the campaign. Only around 100,000 survived to return home.

DAMAGE LIMITATION

The very next day after returning home, Napoleon turned his attention to making excuses. For domestic consumption, he concocted the story that the arrival of a sudden – and totally unexpected – cold spell had prevented an otherwise certain victory. He knew however, that the European powers would be much harder to convince. He had failed in Spain; He had failed in Russia and he understood that they would be looking at him as a failure now, weak and vulnerable. The wolves would soon be circling. That same day, Napoleon also started rebuilding his army, calling up more and more young conscripts for what he was sure was about to descend on him.

REPERCUSSIONS

Friends and foes alike knew exactly what had happened with the Russian campaign and started to react. Prussia withdrew from its alliance with France on Christmas Day 1812. In March 1813, they declared war. Next to desert Napoleon was the Papacy. The Church withdrew its understanding with France. Even Austria, to whom Napoleon was now related by marriage, started looking hostile, rearming themselves as if for war while the Austrian Emperor refused to talk to Napoleon directly any more.

Across Europe, nations were now drawing together a Sixth Coalition. Prussia, Austria, Sweden, Russia, Great Britain, Spain, and Portugal all came together with one aim – to eliminate the threat of Napoleon once and for all.

PRUSSIA

In March 1813, Sweden declared war on France. Prussia followed suit. Coalition forces first sought to open a way across the River Elbe and into France by eliminating the French Forces stationed at Magdeburg. Getting wind of their plan, the French came out to meet them with 10,000 men. In early April, the two armies clashed in a series of conflicts known collectively as the Battle of Möckern. The French were driven back. In another conflict in Vehlitz, (a crossing on the Ehle River), a combined Prussian-Russian force also dislodged French forces in a scrappy battle in which artillery could not be brought to bear and which saw much hand to hand fighting, sometimes waged waist deep in swampy water. The French withdrew back to Magdeburg.

Napoleon's response was swift. He took personal command and led his troops himself on a Spring offensive. In person, he now looked tired, pallid and podgy, so much so that his men started saying *'isn't he looking well?'* in an effort to boost their own morale. Back in fickle Paris, they started to refer to him as 'the China Pig'.

Napoleon slammed into Coalition forces at Lützen and Bautzen, in heavy engagements that cost some 40,000 casualties on both sides. The two battles were the largest yet seen in the Napoleonic Wars with each involving over 250,000 troops. Napoleon won both battles, but lack of proper cavalry meant he could not capitalise on his victories. He had still not been able to replace all the horses slaughtered and eaten in Russia...

Exhausted, both sides were grateful for a temporary armistice. They would use the time to rest and rebuild their forces – and Napoleon would try to get more horses from somewhere. On 26 June, Napoleon met with Klemens von Metternich, minor royal and Foreign Minister of Austria, to try and sort out the question of continuing Austrian neutrality. Metternich was not impressed by Napoleon's recent victories nor his attempts to dominate the meeting. He was told in no uncertain terms that if wanted to keep Austria neutral, he would have to give up the German states and retreat to behind the Rhine once more. This was so unacceptable to Napoleon that he began bellowing at Metternich before taking off his hat and hurling it across the room. He then rounded on the startled minister and told him that he would gladly see another million of his men die than ever agree to such terms. Metternich took his leave with the parting words, *'Sire, you are a lost man...'*

Austria declared war with France in August 1813. Austria, after all, spoke German. For all his actions, Napoleon had only succeeded in bringing the scattered German states closer and closer to each other.

THE BATTLE OF LEIPZIG

During the armistice, Napoleon frantically built up the strength of his forces to some 450,000 men (with another 220,000 reserves). Prussia too was desperately rearming and reorganising their army to meet him. Napoleon wanted nothing more than to settle things his way – with one colossal, decisive battle.

At first things seemed to go Napoleon's way. He inflicted a crushing defeat on the Coalition at Dresden on 26-27 August, killing 40,000 Coalition troops for just 10,000 of his own. However, once again lack of cavalry preventing him from capitalising on his gains. In other battles fought across Germany, the Coalition achieved some notable victories too. It would all come down to Leipzig...

The Battle of Leipzig took four full days to play out. Napoleon's forces in the area around the city numbered some 180,000. The Coalition fielded 350,000. There were no brilliant stratagems employed on either side. The two massive armies engaged and simply fought it out in and around the city. At the end of the final day Napoleon was forced to withdraw. He had suffered 100,000 casualties, many of them just raw conscripts, and had another 30,000 taken as prisoners including 30 French generals. He also lost a further 5,000 men who simply deserted to the enemy side. The Coalition suffered 54,000 casualties. As Napoleon fell back on France, he left another 100,000 men in garrisons scattered about German soil.

All surrendered.

THE NAPOLEONIC WARS

Battle of Leipzig at the Wachau Heights by V.I. Moshkov

Declaration of victory after the Battle of Leipzig, by Johann Peter Krafft

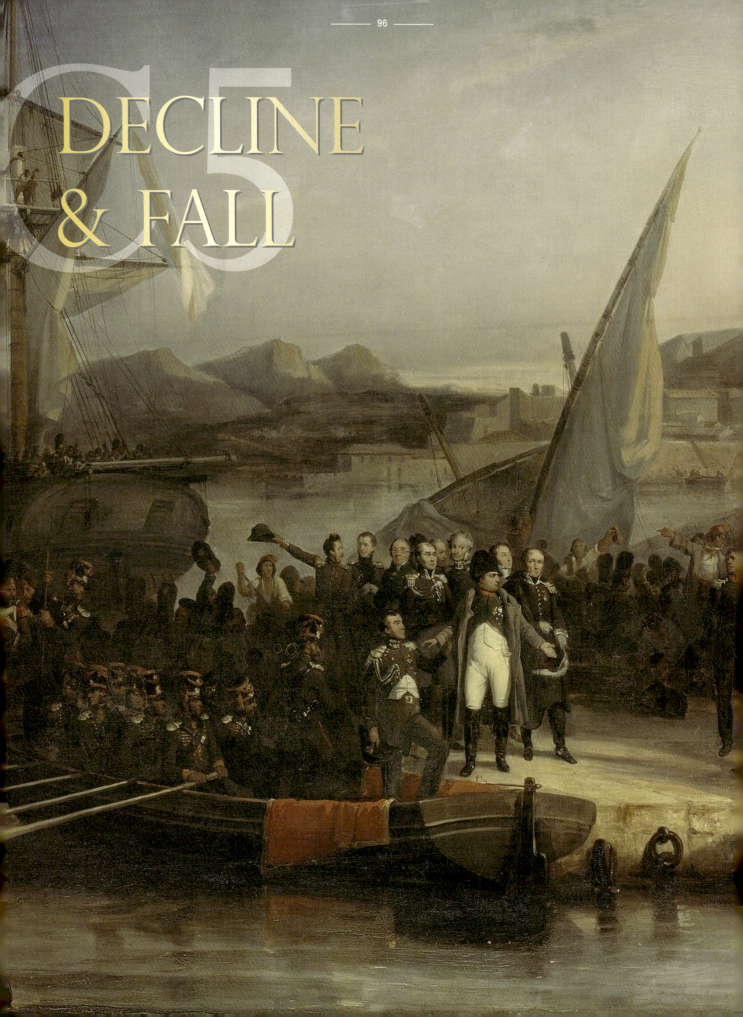

DECLINE & FALL

05

WAR COMES TO FRANCE

An uneasy sort-of peace descended on Spain in late 1812, with the French largely staying out of the way – but poised to strike-up in the Pyrenees. Wellington found his troops starting to rebel against him as conditions for the Coalition Army grew more difficult over the winter. The drenching rain seemed unending, the troops did not have proper winter clothes and desertion grew rife. At one point over 12,000 British soldiers were listed as absent without leave. The Spanish fighting contingent in particular had poor supplies and were starting to starve, leading to fears that they might become totally out of control and attack their fellow countrymen in the towns and villages and on the farms.

In May 1813, Wellington launched a new offensive, leading 120,000 troops out of Portugal into what remained of French-occupied Spain. On 21 June, Wellington's army of 80,000 met and defeated a French force of 66,000 led by Napoleon's brother Joseph at the battle of Vitoria and chased the surviving French cavalry all the way back to the Pyrenees. Joseph Bonaparte only narrowly escaped capture.

Arthur Wellesley, 1st Duke of Wellington

Duke of Wellington crossing the Pyrenees

DECLINE & FALL

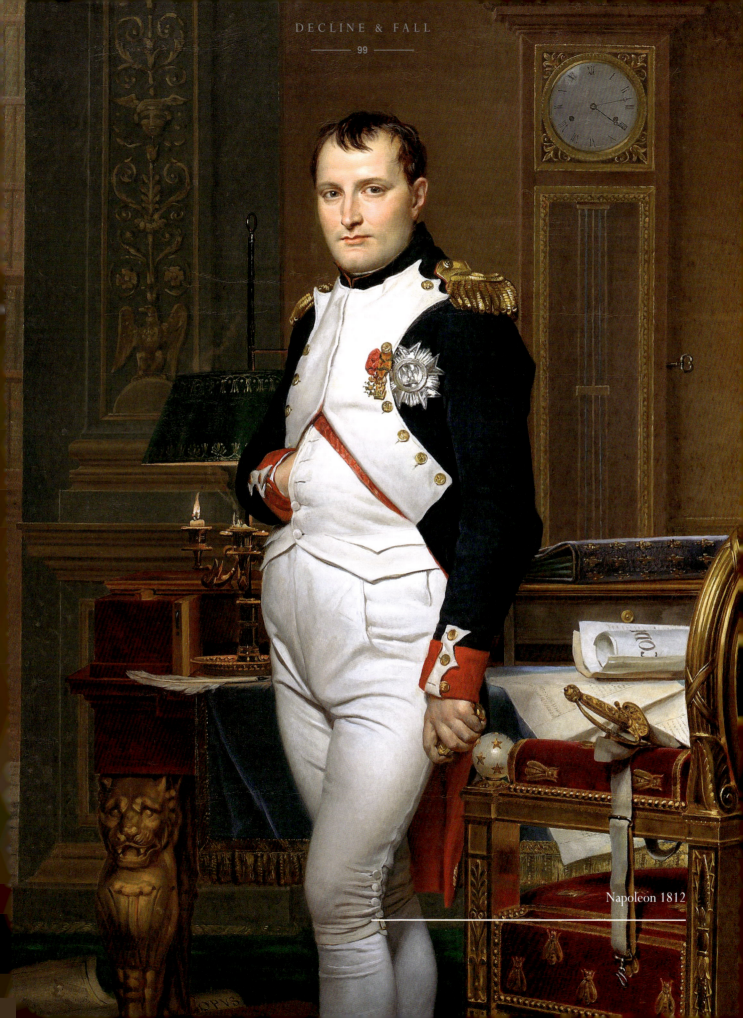

Napoleon 1812

Map of the Battle of the Nive

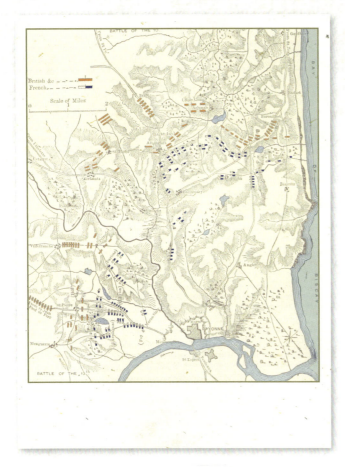

In the summer of 1813, the French did try to reinvade, but were held at a cost of 10,000 men. Wellington then counter-attacked moving north, with thoughts of invading France itself from its vulnerable underbelly. Elsewhere, mopping up campaigns were fought to drive the French out of their remaining Spanish conquests. The French resisted – but all the while Napoleon kept withdrawing more and more troops to use elsewhere.

Now Wellington pushed north, forcing Marshal Soult into a fighting retreat through the Pyrenees. At the Battle of Bidassoa on 7 October 1813, British forces with their Spanish and Portuguese allies made a surprise river crossing, overran the French defensive lines and gained a foothold in France itself. Just over a month later on 10 November, the French were pushed further back still into their own country. December saw another victory for the Coalition at the Battle of the Nive. German troops loyal to Napoleon received news of his defeat at Leipzig and defected en masse to the Coalition and Soult, who had gone on the offensive, was now forced to resume his fighting retreat once more.

Battle of Bidassoa

Marshal Soult

It was the ferociously bad weather, rather than the French, that halted Wellington's advance in the first two months of 1814. When he could finally move again, Wellington left the task of sealing up the garrison at Bayonne to his subordinates and resumed the chase after Soult. In secret, Wellington was worried that his Spanish allies might exact their revenge on the French civilians and had most of them sent home. British troops were subjected to iron handed discipline to ensure they left the innocent well alone. In the event, it was the French troops who plundered and murdered their own kinfolk, as discipline in the ranks started to come apart. The people in the region were very largely Basques, didn't speak French and were considered *'fair game'*. Soult tried to stop the violence, making looting a hanging offenses but it proved futile.

On 27 February, Wellington achieved yet another victory at Orthez. What began as yet another orderly retreat this time turned into a rout. A significant number of French troops ran and never came back again. Moving east now, Wellington fought a number of engagements against Soult's men, forcing him to give up the port of Bordeaux (The third largest city in France) and to take his remaining forces and fall back further to the city of Toulouse.

Short of men, Wellington did not close on Toulouse until Easter Sunday – 10 April 1814. Initially fighting went very badly for the Coalition and they took heavy casualties. Fortunately Soult then decided to abandon the city with his army, frightened by news of Coalition cavalry reinforcements being brought up. He left the Coalition forces to simply march in and occupy it on 12 April. Their entry into the city was cheered by hordes of French monarchists who no longer had to hide their old loyalties. It was while here in Toulouse that Wellington was to hear historic news...

Napoleon and his staff are retuning from Soissons after the Battle of Laon 1814

REVENGE

'La Patrie en Danger'
Napoleon's rallying cry

'Mon dieu... Cossacks in the Rue Racine!'
Mme de Staël

As 1813 turned into 1814, Napoleon's forces had tumbled out of Germany and were now all back in France. He had an army of less than 70,000 he could call on to protect the nation. The Coalition forces, now massing in Germany, could easily boast three times that number.

Mme de Staël

In mid-January 1814, Coalition forces streamed across the border heading directly for Paris in the teeth of a ferocious snowstorm. Prussian forces came in from the north, and Austrian and Russian armies from the east, having recently taken Switzerland. As they went, the Coalition forces burned, pillaged and raped with abandon. Now it was the turn of the French civilian population to experience all the horrors of total war.

Determined to fight to the last, Napoleon personally led the troops remaining at his disposal on a campaign that ran from 10-15 February 1814, which became known as The Six Days Campaign. Outnumbered almost two to one, he nevertheless won four victories over the Prussians of the Army of Silesia in quick succession, inflicting over 17,000 casualties. Their commander, the elderly Field Marshal Blücher, simply had no answer to the speed with which Napoleon could move and manoeuvre his men. It was only the arrival of the army of the King of Bohemia on its way to Paris which forced Napoleon to break off and intercept them in turn rather than finish off the Prussians completely. Nevertheless, mauled and bloody, the entire Army of Silesia was forced to retreat. They would not stop until they had reached safety over the German border.

It was the battle of Battle of Arcis-sur-Aube on 20 March which brought the truth of the situation to Napoleon. The Coalition fielded 80,000 men. Napoleon could barely muster 28,000 to meet them. The French only just managed to extricate themselves from the battlefield and escape.

Faced with an almost impossible decision, Napoleon elected not to try to defend Paris but instead moved what forces he had left to him to the east out of harm's way. The Coalition leaders were tempted to pursue and destroy him, but after a hasty meeting decided to occupy Paris instead. As refugees streamed in from the countryside, the city braced itself for assault, Napoleon's wife Marie-Louise decided to run off back to Austria with their son and much of the French crown jewels. Napoleon's brother Joseph also sloped off disguised as a refugee.

The first barrage of cannons against Paris started up on 30 March, as French officers were busy throwing the lunatics out of Parisian asylums to convert them into makeshift hospitals. Napoleon had given orders to blow up the main powder magazine, which would have taken with it a decent chunk of the city, but he was ignored. Napoleon's commanders Marmont and Mortier tried to defend the city with what meagre sources they had ranged on the heights of Montmartre, but the outcome was never in doubt. The city was surrendered on 31 March 1814 and rapidly occupied by 150,000 Coalition troops. Although Cossacks were seen riding up and down

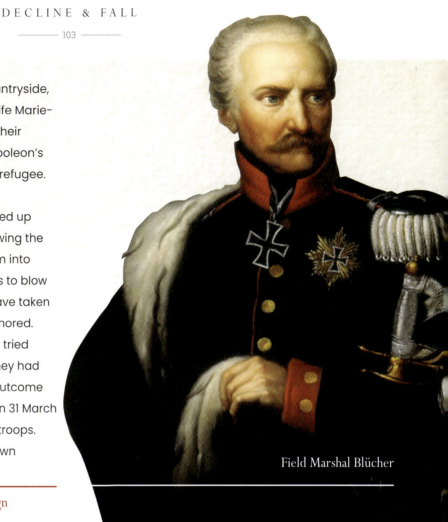

Field Marshal Blücher

The Battle of Montmirail part of the 6 Day Campaign

The Cossacks in Paris 1814

the Champs Élysées, the worst aspects of the horrors inflicted on the peasantry were not repeated. The city was not sacked. Instead, order was swiftly restored and plans drawn up for the return of the French monarchy. Napoleon tried desperately to convince his commanders to march immediately on Paris to save it, but he was overruled. France had fallen. And Napoleon with it.

Instead, they insisted that Napoleon would have to go into exile on the island of Elba and his son would inherit nothing. Napoleon took the deal and, on 28 April, he stepped aboard the British warship HMS *Undaunted* that would take him out to his place of banishment. By the time he arrived on 4 May, Napoleon had already completed sketches for the new flag he would give his island. It had bees on it.

EXILE

Even Napoleon had to concede that he had been resoundingly beaten and, on 6 April 1814, he formally surrendered and looked around for peace terms. Previous terms now seemed incredibly generous, but they were off the table now. Napoleon suggested that he be allowed to stay in France and that his little son should become Emperor. The Coalition rejected that out of hand.

ELBA

The Island of Elba was a tiny speck in the Mediterranean just over six miles off the Tuscan coast. It measured just 19 miles long by 7 miles wide, 12,000 people called it home and it was remarkable only for its obscurity. Napoleon had been awarded a grand new title for the occasion of his arrival – that of

View from the garden of the Palazzina dei Mulini in Portoferraio

'Emperor and Ruler of Elba' – and was probably the only one who didn't see that this was a snide joke by the Coalition. He took it seriously.

Napoleon set to work ruling his new empire from his palace (once an old mill) in the island's capital, Portoferraio, using his 600-strong personal bodyguard and a retinue of 400 other troops to enforce his will on the bemused islanders. He had ambitious plans for his new empire (including annexing even smaller islands nearby) but unfortunately for him the French government reneged on their promise to send him two million francs a year, so his miniature empire was constantly short of cash. With what he had, he dabbled in local government reform and improving the islander's infrastructure. All the reasonably priced projects were

Napoleon at Fontainebleau by Paul Delaroche, 1814

completed in just a few months, leaving Napoleon angry, bitter, bored and dangerously close to broke.

Napoleon's 64-year-old mother Letizia came to live with him, but all she did was remind him that she had always predicted his downfall and he had only himself to blame for the trouble he had got himself into. This did not improve his mood. When she was not criticizing her son, she made good use of his billiards table for hours at a time or else would accuse Napoleon of cheating her at cards. He tried to persuade Marie-Louise to come and live with him, but she refused, preferring to run off with an Austrian general. Josephine died while he was in exile. Surly, fat and dozy now, Napoleon struggled to assuage his boredom and frustration. He started renovating his palace just for something to do and returned to his old love of gardening.

Wealthy young British travellers on their 'Grand Tour' of Europe would now divert to Elba in the hope of seeing the once great emperor pottering in his garden or strolling the streets. Those lucky enough to meet him were surprised that he was actually quite convivial with them. He talked freely and asked

British satirical cartoons of Napoleon's exile

lots of questions about things in the outside world. Underneath the veneer of civility, however, he began to feel that he was now some sort of circus freak to be stared at through the bars of his cage. One British writer fortunate enough to talk with Napoleon thought he saw the mask slip and later reported that '*I doubt not that he breathed vengeance within himself against us for having come to see him in his humility.*'

Back home, the old Bourbon monarchy ruled once more, with the grossly fat and quite ridiculous Louis XVIII on the throne. France had entered yet another recession and was experiencing hunger and deprivation once more. Royalists sought revenge on Republicans, Catholics used the opportunity to oppress Protestants and Napoleon received floods of letters begging him to come home and save La Belle France once more – or at least he said he did. A bored Napoleon was a dangerous Napoleon.

ESCAPE

'Satan rising from the sulphurous fog…'
Robert Southey

"A thousand ideas and projects are formed; resistance is nowhere decided…'I shall arrive before any plan has been organized against me.
Napoleon

By mid-February 1815, Napoleon was truly sick of Elba and determined to return home, seize the French nation and pursue his true destiny once more. On 26 February, he jumped on a Frigate and set off back home with his meagre troops and a million francs worth of gold. He returned on 1 March strutting down the gang plank at the small south-eastern French port of Antibes.

Return from the island of Elba, February 28, 1815

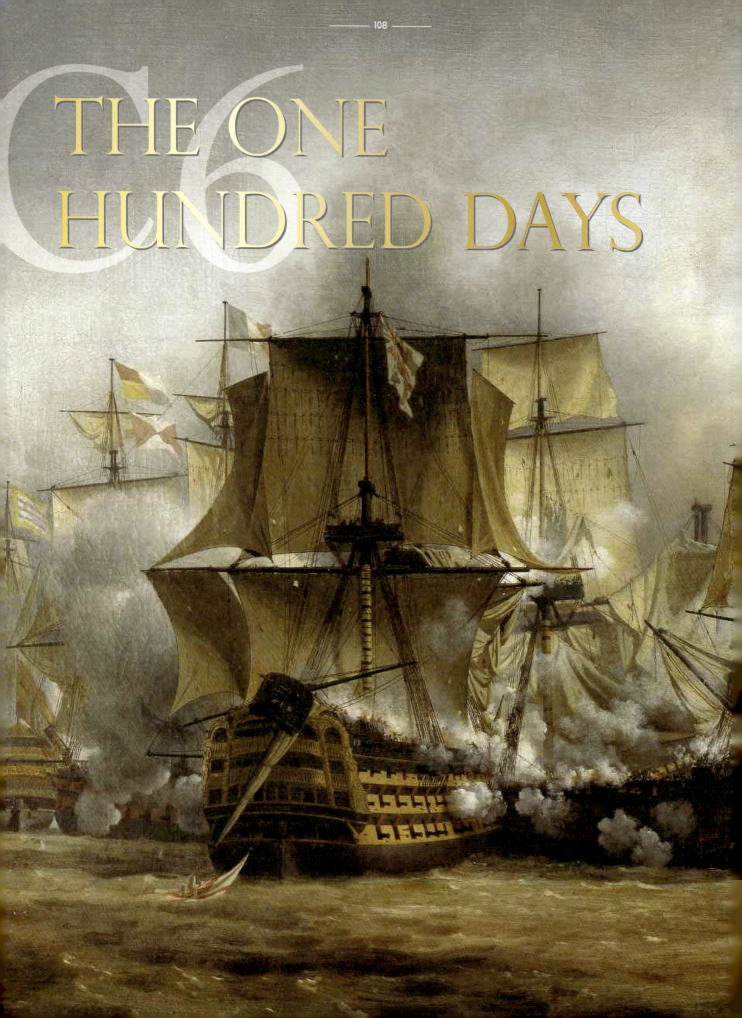

C6 THE ONE HUNDRED DAYS

THE ONE HUNDRED DAYS THAT WEREN'T

Thus began the period modern historians refer to as 'The 100 Days', the time between Napoleon's return to France and meeting his fate. Someone miscounted. Napoleon actually enjoyed 111 days to once again pursue his destiny.

Marshal Ney

HOME

'Soldiers, your general, called to the throne by the choice of the people, and raised on your shields, has come back to you. Come and join him! I am sprung from the Revolution. I am come to save the people from the slavery into which priests and nobles would plunge them.'
Napoleon

'Why is bread dearer and meat cheaper since 20 March? Because the baker has left and the butcher has returned'
Parisian joke, 1815.

At the port, Napoleon was met by the local health inspector who tried to have him arrested for breaking customs regulations, but that was the only opposition he met.

Napoleon swiftly moved north, with his little army at his back. Everywhere he went, he spread stories that he would be bring radical new reforms to the French people, together with new financial benefits. Oddly, he also offered peace. By and large, the people supported him. Aware that he was coming, the new French authorities sent out a force to meet him on the road, with Marshal Ney in charge. Ney promised to return a defeated Napoleon in an iron cage for his majesty's pleasure.

Reaching the outskirts of Grenoble on 5 March, where hostile forces from the 5th Infantry Regiment lay in wait at Laffrey, he stepped out between the two opposing armies at sunset while his musicians played the Marseillaise for dramatic effect. He ripped open his greatcoat and shouted, *'It is I, Napoleon. Kill your emperor if you wish.'* There was at first a confused muttering from the soldiers ranged against him, then a few shouts of *'Long live the Emperor!'* Napoleon then told an outrageous lie. He said*, 'The forty-five wisest men in the Paris government have summoned me from Elba to put France to rights. My return is backed by the three leading powers in Europe!'*

They believed him, and the cries of *'Long Live the Emperor'* rose to a deafening crescendo as muskets were thrown aside and clattered to the ground. Needless to say, the entire force defected to him. A day later, the men of the 7th Infantry declared their loyalty to Napoleon too. Grenoble fell, followed by Lyon. He moved on. Civilians at Villefranche painted their homes red, white and blue to salute him, and even saved the remains of his chicken dinner as relics to be treasured.

At Auxerre on 14 March, Napoleon finally came face to face with Marshal Ney, the man who had sworn to cage him. Instead, Ney joined him and the two rode together at the head of an ever-growing column towards Paris. Ney's force of 6,000 men went with them, their loyalty now sworn to Napoleon. Travelling through a land of ever-shifting loyalties, Napoleon reserved his deepest distrust for the ordinary people – the rabble. He loved them as an abstract, bent to his will, but feared them as human beings for their ignorance and animal stupidity. Ney understood this and had begged Napoleon in a letter to stop acting the tyrant and instead devote himself to the happiness of the French People. Napoleon tore Ney's latter up and told the Marshal he was insane.

When he got the news, Louis XVIII fled. He moved so fast that he forgot to pack his slippers.

THE CONGRESS OF VIENNA

Also aware that Napoleon was on his way were the grandees of Europe. They had assembled in Vienna for a congress to decide the future borders of the European nations in a post-Napoleonic world.

French political cartoons

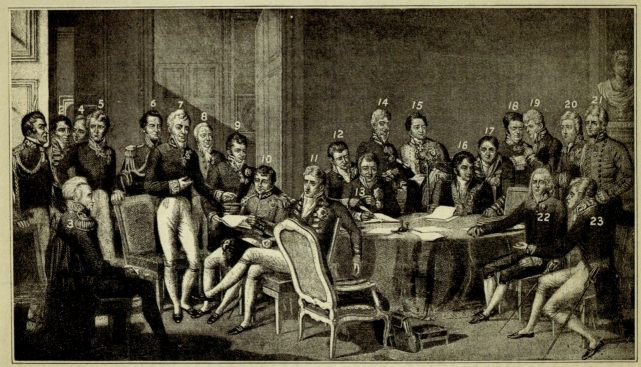

THE CONGRESS OF VIENNA, 1814-'5, WHICH READJUSTED THE MAP OF EUROPE AFTER THE NAPOLEONIC WARS

1, Wellington; 2, Lobo; 3, Hardenberg; 4, Saldanha; 5, Lowenhielm; 6, Noailles; 7, Metternich; 8, Dupin; 9, Nesselrode; 10, Palmella; 11, Castlereagh; 12, Dalberg; 13, Wessenberg; 14, Rasoumoffsky; 15, Stewart; 16, Labrador; 17, Clancarty; 18, Wacken; 19, Gentz; 20, Humboldt; 21, Cathcart; 22, Talleyrand; 23, Stackelberg. The dominating figures at the Congress were Prince Metternich, the Austrian Minister of State, who acted as President of the Congress; Prince Talleyrand, the French diplomat; Castlereagh and Wellington, representing Great Britain; Hardenberg and Humboldt, from Prussia; and Nesselrode, from Russia.

Members of The Congress Of Vienna

The talks had been so fractious that one or two of the Coalition allies almost declared war on each other during the talks and Czar Alexander actually challenged the Austrian Foreign Minister Metternich to a duel. There had also been widespread talk that, whilst Napoleon was in exile on Elba, he was still a major threat. Some argued that he should be sent further away, perhaps to the Azores or the island of St Helena off the coast of Africa. Still others argued that he should be executed or assassinated. No one was in the mood to deal with a resurgent Napoleon. Within just four days of his arrival back home, they had him declared an outlaw and started making plans to finish him once and for all. The major powers promised a truly staggering commitment of troops – over half a million dedicated to the task. The Seventh Coalition was announced at once.

Czar Alexander

PARIS

'If a nation wants happiness, it must obey orders and remain silent.'
Napoleon

'He has reappeared - this madman dyed with our blood! He is another Attila, another Genghis Khan, but more terrible and more hateful
Journal des Débats

On 20 March 1815, Napoleon's military column entered Paris. No one tried to stop them. Instead, crowds of Parisians gathered to cheer him in as he retook up residence at the Tuileries. Napoleon had already annulled the existing French government in a speech given at Lyon on 13 March. Now he wasted no time in getting down to drawing up a new constitution for France and even made some noises about declaring himself King rather than Emperor. On 1 June he opened a new bicameral French parliament, which would naturally be entirely subordinate to him in all things.

And all the while France trembled in anticipating of old scores being settled and civil war. The mob wanted arming. The Jacobites wanted the political right slaughtered to the last man and the rightist Royalists wanted a greater role for the absent Monarchy. Nothing it seemed had been settled. The old enmities remained, and Napoleon struggled to contain them. All the factions feared that another war was coming and that Napoleon, in his madness would set them against the European powers once more, getting their remaining sons butchered in the process. Napoleon's contempt for their fears lost him many of those who had once supported him, as did his plans to raise taxes upon them. France no longer had any

Departure of the allies of the Congress of Vienna to the battlefield to stop the advance of the French army, May 29, 1815

conquered nations to plunder. The money would have to come from the French people. They would in effect, be paying for their own children's executions as Napoleon set off in pursuit of glory once more.

Napoleon also discovered that the Bourbon King had cut deep into the standing army to save money and he had barely 46,000 troops ready to fight should the Coalition attack. By May, he had swelled this number back up to 198,000 (often with returning French prisoners of war) with another 66,000 in various stages of training. At the same time, he made peace overtures to the Coalition, promising to stay within French borders this time. They were in no mood to listen. After all, he had broken just about every treaty he had ever signed. This was going to end.

Napoleon had two choices. He realised he was going to have to fight, but should he opt for a defensive or offensive campaign. Defensive campaigns had never suited him and he had very bad memories of the last time he had fought to defend France. So he would go on the offensive.

THE ROAD TO WATERLOO

Both sides mobilised as fast as they could. Wellington favoured going on the attack in June 1815 but as the Austrians and particularly the Russians were finding it slow and difficult to mobilise, the grand assault on France would have to be held up until late July. Then it was intended, the Coalition would surge into France with an overwhelming force of 700,000 men. The Coalition would attack Napoleon from three different directions; British, Dutch and Prussian forces would march from the north out of Belgium, the Austrians would come through the Alps and Austro-Russian forces would surge over the Rhine. It was all planned.

But Napoleon proved quicker. Taking his Army of the North, comprising 120,000 troops and 360 cannon, he headed north to confront the British and Prussian troops in Belgium. His plan was to drive a wedge between the two Coalition armies and then deal with them one at a time. The rest of his forces – some 180,000 strong - would be sent to guard the other borders. Napoleon only had a few Marshals to choose from now as he selected his commanders. Some had defected to the enemy and some had remained loyal to the king in hiding. Two Marshals also went into hiding by themselves to avoid what was to come. He appointed his veteran of Spain Marshal Soult to be his chief of staff. He was not Napoleon's first choice, but the officer who was refused to serve. Soult had no experience in such a role. Marshal Ney was given command of the Army of the North's left flank, despite concerns about his mental health and his overall intelligence. No one doubted his courage, but the Russian Campaign had taken its toll on him. Grouchy took command of the Right wing. His problem was that while he was an excellent infantry commander, he had little experience of commanding and using cavalry. Napoleon would take personal command of the centre.

Facing him, Wellington commanded 100,000 troops (Nominally British, but with strong German and Dutch components) and 200 cannon presently stationed close to Brussels and Field Marshall Blücher (now 72 years old) could call on 130,000 soldiers and 300 guns and had been positioned in the locality of Namur. Their plan was to join forces on the Belgian border in July and then race for Paris.

Napoleon's rapid move north up the main road to Brussels caught both Coalition armies completely by surprise. A shocked Wellington quickly moved west,

THE ONE HUNDRED DAYS

Napoleon, 1815

so that he could be closer to the Channel ports if he needed to evacuate. The result was to move the two Coalition armies further apart, just as Napoleon wanted.

Prussian and French forces first battled at a river crossing over the Sambre at Charleroi on 15 June and then Ligny on 16 June. Ligny proved to be vicious and bloody with each side losing close to 20,000 men. By nightfall, the Prussians had been defeated and were retreating north under the cover of a violent thunderstorm. It was to be Napoleon's final victory. Meanwhile, Wellington was establishing strong defensive positions at Quatre Bras. They were attacked by Ney on 16 June, but held firm. Marshal Ney had been suffering one of his manic-depressive episodes and was singularly unmotivated, while Napoleon too was suffering with haemorrhoids and could not get up the enthusiasm to chase the Prussians until the afternoon of the 17th – by which time it was too late to achieve much.

That same afternoon, Wellington left his positions at Quatre Bras in order to reposition north closer to Blücher. He chose the village of Waterloo.

WATERLOO

'Wellington is a bad general, the English are bad troops and it will be a picnic'
Napoleon, before Waterloo

Sunday, 18 June 1815.

Wellington's forces were mostly positioned behind a three mile long ridge, with a road running down the middle. He had established a strong position. To the fore were three strongpoints, Papelotte to the left, La Haye Sainte in the centre and Hougoumont Chateau on the right. A special force of troops had been positioned west out by Braine L'Alleud in case Napoleon tried one of his grand flanking manoeuvres. There were some 68,000 Coalition troops on the field with 184 guns. The majority were to the right. Wellington had ordered Blücher to race to join him and reinforce his left.

Two miles away, the French were slow to stir and it took them until 12 noon to position their 72,000 soldiers and 266 guns, partly due to a thunderstorm during the night which had soaked and softened the

THE ONE HUNDRED DAYS

British commander Wellington receives the message that help from Prussian troops is underway. Bottom left the wounded Prince of Orange is being carried away

The Battle of Waterloo By William Sadler

Royal North British Dragoons' Sergeant Charles Ewart defending the seized standard of the French 45th Regiment of the Line from a French lancer during the Battle of Waterloo, 18 June 1815

battleground. Their aim was to launch a diversionary strike against Hougoumont, thereby sucking in Wellington's reserves and weakening the British centre. The centre would then be attacked and dealt a crushing blow. By nightfall, Napoleon was confident, he would be leading his men triumphantly into Brussels.

Napoleon was suffering that day from his haemorrhoids, which meant he could not ride around on his horse during the battle. He would have to delegate more responsibility to his commanders than he ever felt comfortable doing.

Things started to go wrong for Napoleon almost right away. As battle commenced, infantry under Napoleon's brother Jérôme launched their diversionary assault against Hougoumont. However, fighting against 400 light infantry from the King's German Legion, and then reinforcements from the Coldstream Guards and the Scots Guards, they failed to take the building as had been intended. Fighting around Hougoumont would continue all day.

Blücher was already on the move to join Wellington. Grouchy attacked his forces at Wavre hoping to delay him, but his attack was blunted and contained. 89,000 Prussians continued marching on Waterloo. By 1.30pm, Napoleon got wind of the Prussian advance and sent orders for Grouchy's forces to return to Waterloo to reinforce him.

Ney led the grand attack against the British centre, but the ranks held. Their fire first stopped and then broke the French. They retreated, pursued by a contingent of Coalition cavalry 2,000 strong. Unfortunately for Wellington, his cavalry then went after Napoleon's 'grand battery of cannon' and were in turn driven off by French lancers with heavy casualties. Wellington was later to complain

General Emmanuel de Grouchy

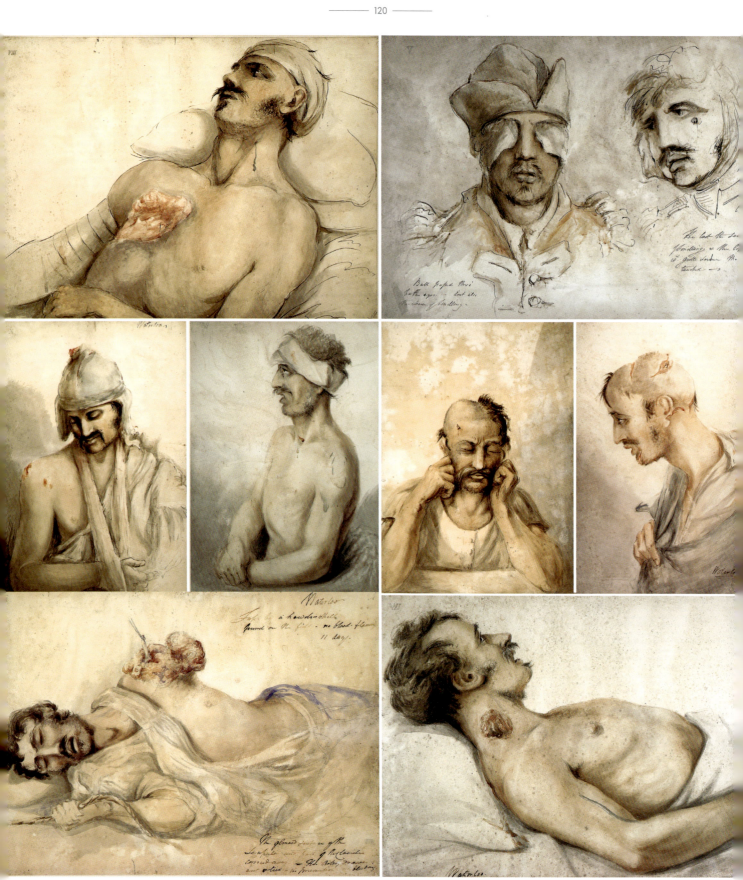

Studies of Waterloo wounded by Surgeon Charles Bell

'Our officers of cavalry have acquired a trick of galloping at everything. They never consider the situation, never think of manoeuvring before an enemy, and never keep back or provide a reserve'. With his first thrust a failure, Ney then tried to seize the British strongpoint of La Haye Sainte. He was again driven back. A short while later, he mistakenly thought that the British were withdrawing from the centre and personally led a powerful cavalry force of some 84 squadrons in total to rout them. He was wrong. The British infantry simply formed twenty defensive squares as the shout went up, *'prepare to receive cavalry!'* The French cavalry simply couldn't penetrate or do much damage to the infantry squares, receiving withering fire as they tried to smash them apart. More cavalry were thrown into the already failing assault, then more still. The squares were charged a dozen times but held firm each time. Each time the French cavalry retreated to regroup, they were harassed by Coalition cavalry and pounded by artillery.

By 4pm, all French reserves had been committed. At 6pm, Napoleon ordered Ney to assault La Haye Sainte once more. This time the French attack succeeded in sweeping the British from the farm compound.

French guns were at last brought up to pound the British defensive squares in the centre. Ney asked for reinforcements to launch an assault but it was not until 7.15pm that Napoleon felt able to commit them. Ney received some of Napoleon's finest troops, the men of the Middle Guard. In eleven years of fighting for Napoleon, they had never failed to take their objective. Ney intended them to march straight down the centre, but for some reason they veered off and attacked Wellington's right of centre instead. They walked straight into the massed fire from several of Wellington's units. Ten minutes of concentrated fire smashed them, and they retreated for the first time ever. French morale began to crack.

Now units of newly arrived Prussian artillery started pounding the French ranks. At the same time, their fresh and unbloodied troops slammed into the French on the right flank. All around Napoleon, soldiers were streaming past him in headlong panic. Soon, he was running with them in his coach. Grouchy's units followed soon after.

Napoleon's force took 33,000 casualties on the field of Waterloo that day. The allies 22,000.

French Cuirassiers charging onto the British squares during the Battle of Waterloo. by Henri Félix Emmanuel Philippoteaux

Battle Of Waterloo by Clément-Auguste Andrieux

The ravine of Waterloo, oil on canvas by Ulpiano Checa

Assault on the village of Plancenoit during the Battle of Waterloo on June 18, 1815 by Ludwig Elsholtz

AFTERMATH

'My heart is broken by the terrible loss I have sustained in my old friends and companions and my poor soldiers. Believe me, nothing except a battle lost can be half so melancholy as a battle won.'

Wellington

Wellington did not sleep in his bed the night after Waterloo; someone was dying in it. He ate by himself and tumbled exhausted onto a temporary pallet without bothering to wash first. He was woken early by a doctor with a list of casualties, and cried as he read the list.

As Napoleon rode frantically for Paris, his carriage was surrounded by truly hellish scenes. However, Napoleon was a veteran of sixty battles; he'd seen it all before and remained quite unperturbed. He was plotting. Under the moonlight, the entire world seemed to stink of putrefaction and gun smoke. It seemed too as if every mouth in the world was screaming as field hospitals along the roadside desperately tended to the most seriously wounded – usually by amputation without aneasthetic. Everywhere men were fleeing south, being hunted down by squadrons of Prussian cavalry and butchered with lance and sabre if they were found. The wounded who had managed to escape the battlefield walked or crawled in the mud until Belgian peasants set upon them and robbed them. If they resisted, they were murdered. No-one would notice. Riderless horses galloped through the fields of wheat and barley, so frightened that they ran themselves to death and died, thrashing amidst the crops.

Looting had begun even during the battle, as men rifled their dead or wounded companions' pockets for valuables during any lull in the fighting. As night fell on the battlefield, locals came to take what was left, often stripping off uniforms for the cloth and leaving the corpse naked. Finally came those who traded in false teeth, to wrench out the teeth from the mouths of corpse to use in dentures. In the end, those Coalition dead who remained on the field of conflict were manoeuvred into giant pits by long-handled pitchforks. It is said that the pits filled up so deep that arms and ghastly open-jawed faces protruded from the soil after the pits were covered over. French corpses were heaved onto giant pyres and simply burned.

And still Napoleon refused to accept defeat…

Wellington

THIRD TIME LUCKY?

' (Napoleon's) whole life, civil, political and military, was a fraud'.
The Duke of Wellington

'(Napoleon) came back to Paris like a fugitive, thinking only of his person…the magic is gone.'
Pierre Fontaine

Pierre Fontaine

Napoleon was barely back to Paris on 21 June before he was drawing up plans to relaunch the war. The first thing he need was hundreds of thousands of new troops. Mass conscription seemed the obvious answer.

He also took time to write his own, unique, account of the Battle of Waterloo. He had, apparently, won it:

'After eight hours of firing and infantry and cavalry charges, the whole (French) army was able to look with satisfaction upon a battle won and the battlefield in our possession.'

It didn't matter though what he said and did any more. Both the legislature and the people now saw through him and his authority evaporated. On 22 June he abdicated, saying with true nobility, *'I offer myself as a sacrifice to the hatred of France's enemies'* and proclaimed his son as the emperor before moving in to Josephine's old palace in Malmaison three days later to consider his plans. He was totally unused to being irrelevant and as he sat brooding, the Allies entered Paris on 29 June with the aim of restoring the Bourbon Monarchy once more. Louis XVIII returned to his hastily vacated throne the very next day. History does not record whether or not he ever got his slippers back.

Finally, Napoleon received word that Prussian troops had been sent to get him – and no-one minded much if he was brought back dead or alive. Austria intended to have him executed anyway. He fled, going to the port of Rochefort with the aim of jumping on a ship bound for America. *'I could live there with dignity,'* he explained and had his servants pack enough furniture and goods to fill both the American city home and the country mansion he dreamed of. Unfortunately, the

Britain's Prince Regent

Captain Frederick Maitland

Royal Navy was currently blockading every significant French port. There was to be no escape. On 13 July, Napoleon penned what was a grovelling letter to Britain's Prince Regent asking for political asylum. This was against the advice of his confidants who warned him, *'they will treat you as a trophy of Waterloo...'* Now he dreamed of a quiet retirement in London's suburbia. He was refused. Plans were made to smuggle Napoleon out of the besieged port hunched in a rum barrel, but they came to nothing. With French authorities now seeking to arrest him, on July 15, he surrendered himself to Captain Frederick Maitland on the 74-gun *HMS Bellerophon* (Better known in the fleet as *'The Billy Ruffian'.*) He was given the captain's cabin for his quarters. From there he was shipped off to Torbay, where he temporarily became a tourist attraction. Boatloads of locals rowed out for a glimpse of him strutting the deck. Napoleon was never once allowed to tread on English soil.

HMS Bellerophon leaving Torbay with the defeated Emperor Napoleon aboard

Napoleon aboard Bellerophon while off the English coast

ST. HELENA
– EXILE AND ENDINGS

' I have fought sixty battles, and I assure you that I have learned nothing from all of them that I did not know in the first.'
Napoleon

The British knew exactly where Napoleon should go – somewhere where he could do no more harm to the world. St Helena was chosen for his exile. A rock barely 20 miles in circumference 1,000 miles off the coast of West Africa and distinguished only by the number of people who caught amoebic dysentery there. La Belle France would be 5,000 miles away. Here, Napoleon would be well guarded by a permanent garrison of 2,500 Coalition troops and a squadron of frigates stationed offshore, as well as 500 guns pointing out to sea in case some Bonapartists decided on a rescue mission.

Naturally Napoleon protested, claiming that he was now a British citizen with full rights and demanding that he be executed rather than exiled. He even hinted at suicide if he did not get his way, but his words fell on deaf ears. British lawyers sought to have him released on niceties of law, since the legalities of doing anything to an international leader-come-tyrants were not well established. Their efforts might well have worked if the Royal Navy hadn't sailed his prison ship beyond the horizon and left the lawyers impotently waving their legal papers out over an empty sea.

Napoleon was transferred to *HMS Northumberland* on 9 August, all the while grumbling about his legal status as he was taken on board. He was now forty-six years old.

'This is a shameful island,' he said upon first sighting St Helena on 15 October 1815. He was to live in Longwood House, a damp, cold, mildewy, rat-infested and rundown building, which Napoleon saw as a British attempt to murder him before his time. Eventually the luggage which had been packed and intended for life in America,

HMS Bellerophon leaving Torbay with the defeated Emperor Napoleon aboard

turned up on the island and Napoleon was able to make Longwood feel a bit more like home. The brown rats were never properly ejected however and often shared the dining table with Napoleon and his guests come dinner.

He was allowed to take with him some courtiers and twelve servants. Among his courtiers was General Gourgaud, who was outrageously camp and constantly referred to Napoleon as 'she'. He didn't last the course. The little court was a hotbed of jealousy, intrigue and a few affairs. Amongst them, Bonaparte sat down to dictate his memoirs for six hours every day. When he wasn't exaggerating or plain making things up, he tinkered in his garden, sometimes in his dressing gown rediscovering his love of horticulture. His garden became such a thing of joy to him that he personally shot and killed a bullock, a goat and three hens who dared to trespass on it.

He also tried to learn English but found the task far too onerous. He held balls and played cards with English officers. Those who knew him claimed he frequently cheated. At odd times, he would just walk off and stare out to sea. He fantasised being set free by a more liberal British government, hoped to see America

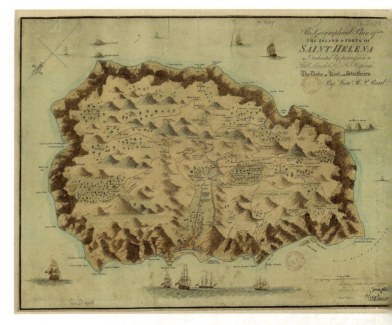

and dreamed of going to South America and forging it himself into another great empire. He also found religion – or at least an interest in it.

Napoleon's chief gaoler was Sir Hudson Lowe, regarded as a fair and conscientious man. When Napoleon found that he could not bribe or otherwise corrupt Lowe, he made him his arch enemy, spreading poisonous rumours and sometimes hurling abuse at him when they met. The scoundrel

Napoleon dictating his memoirs to general Gourgaud, 1820

German political cartoon

was a skilled poisoner, a bandit leader etc etc. Their feud passed the time, and Napoleon was mightily bored. He complained and complained and then complained some more, making Lowe's daily life a living nightmare. He also deliberately vanished several times, making Lowe think he had escaped and causing a great panic. In fact, Napoleon was just hiding in a cupboard or some such. To thwart such mischief, Lowe ordered guards to peer in Napoleon's window at night to check on him and even had a spyhole drilled through the ceiling of his bedroom.

Napoleon's will, which he also drew up on the island, in part read:

'My death is not natural. I have been assasinated by the English Oligarchy and their hired murderer Lowe. The English people will not be long in avenging me.'

In 1820, Napoleon's health started to deteriorate. He became convinced that the British were poisoning him, and had a see-saw constructed in his billiard room which he was convinced would set him on the path to good health once more. It didn't.

He died on 5 May, still talking about Josephine. Doctors attending him concluded that he had been killed by a cancerous ulcer in his stomach, or

Sir Hudson Lowe

Longwood House

else hepatitis, but his true cause of death remains unconfirmed. It is a popular theory today that he died from arsenic poising off of his wallpaper.

He was buried on the island after a small but sincere military funeral with a stone that merely said, *'here lies'* because the French and British could not agree on the appropriate wording. He was dug up again in 1840 and returned to Paris, where he was awarded a magnificent state funeral before being interred in *Les invalides*. By now, the public perception had once more swung in his favour. He was now *'The King of the French'* and a national treasure, instead of a self-centred tyrant who brought abject slaughter and misery to the continent. In Britain, Charlotte Brontë treasured her sliver of Napoleon's coffin. Time, it seems, really does heal all things.

Plaster casting of a Napoleon death mask

THE ONE HUNDRED DAYS

The landing of the ashes of Napoleon I by François Fortuné Antoine Férogio

LEGACY

Napoleon started out actively projecting the idea that he was the very embodiment – on horseback – of the very best ideals of the Revolution. He would sweep away the old tyrannies of the Church, the Monarchy and Aristocracy and replace them throughout Europe with a more fair and egalitarian concept of human values. He would bring Democracy to the repressed – even though he himself did not remotely believe in it. He believed instead in the will of the common man as expressed by one all-powerful leader.

The Intelligencia and the artistic elite of Europe, the thinkers, the poets, the writers, flocked to support him, putting idealism before reality. In a later century, Lenin would refer to such men as *'useful idiots'*. Beethoven for example dedicated his Eroica Symphony to Napoleon. Hegel praised him to the rafters – even after French troops had looted his house. Wordsworth and Coleridge were early sycophantic admirers.

The ordinary men and women of Europe had no such faith. What they experienced was war, pestilence, famine and tyranny wrought by a single man. French forces invaded their lands, their crops were stolen and their women raped and murdered. Their cultural treasures were 'appropriated' for finer minds in Paris to properly appreciate. Their new governments would be nothing more than puppets of the French, exercising progressively harder taxes to help pay for Napoleon's all-devouring war machine. The best job, especially in the bureaucracies, would be hived off to French citizens, and French control further strengthened. Napoleon's secret police would watch them with Gestapo-like hawkishness. For a supposed believer in equality, Napoleon practiced nepotism at every opportunity. Brother Joseph was appointed King of Spain and Lucien King of Holland. Jérôme became King of Westphalia. Sisters too. Eliza was made grand duchess of Tuscany. Caroline became Queen of Naples. The ordinary people knew the truth. It would take until Napoleon crowned himself Emperor for the *'Useful Idiots'* to catch up. Meet the new boss, same as the old boss. In the end, the *'Useful idiots'* turned against Napoleon not merely because he was revealed as just another tyrant, but because of their own fickle tastes. The zeitgeist as turning away from a love of all things old world and classical in favour of pagan Gothic tastes. As if to prove the point, a few scant days after Waterloo, Mary Shelley (Author of Frankenstein) and Lord Byron strode across the battlefield picking up discarded artefacts...

Napoleon's civil and legal reforms had a long lasting effect to be sure, as well as his promotion of the metric system, but all in the end may be worth nothing more than a Gallic shrug.

It is also suggested that Napoleon was an early proponent of a European Union. To be sure he was, but only with him as its sole ruler and Emperor. He never achieved anything like it of course. Instead he only succeeded in uniting much of Europe against himself in a common cause to get rid of him. He did succeed in uniting the German states however, in common cause against him. The Germans in their blood seemed to rather like a dictator figure or two and Napoleon is undoubtedly the grandsire of Adolf Hitler. Mao, Stalin and Mussolini too. He took over a state and turned it into a weapon which he turned not only upon his own people but all those innocent nations around him.

Napoleon ultimately achieved nothing, except for the deaths of millions and the deepest suffering of millions more. But then, he didn't really set out

THE ONE HUNDRED DAYS

to achieve anything except to conquer and be the grand high pooh-bah . France rehabilitated him in later years to the status of national hero, to their shame, and there are those who would still deeply admire him. Perhaps they use the excuse of admiring his 'military genius' when what they really mean is that a rough and ready man who takes things with his own two hands exerts almost a sexual persuasion or a pathetic attempt at vicarious self-actualisation transferal. Adler may have invented the term 'Napoleon Complex' but surely the lingering admiration for Napoleon needs to be looked for in the realms of the Freudian. Weak men dream of being strong men. Strong men get people killed.

Napoleon appears on the horizon on horseback above his armies Oil on canvas by Hans von Faber du Faur

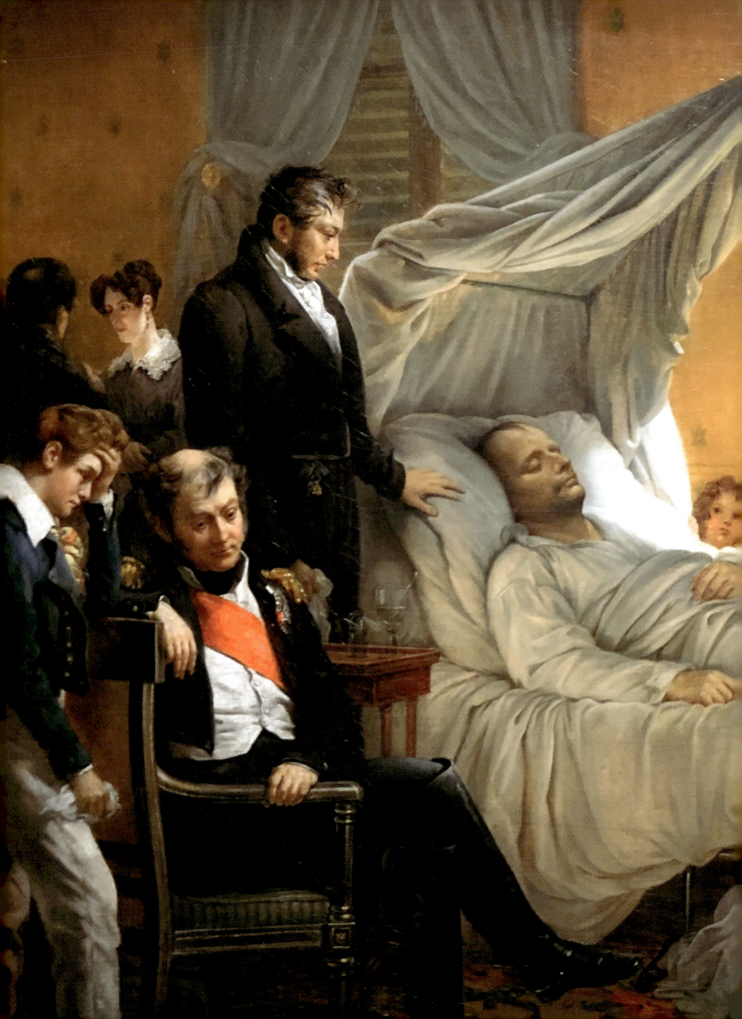